Recipes for Success

A Cookbook from the Warm Springs Rehabilitation Foundation

Dedication

This book is dedicated to the thousands of patients, families, doctors, staff, and employees who have used their own "recipes for success" in dealing with the challenges of injury prevention and physical disability. Over Warm Springs' 60-year history, their steadfast and often heroic efforts are a testament to the enormous healing power of the human spirit.

Published by Warm Springs Rehabilitation Foundation
Copyright© 1997 Warm Springs Rehabilitation Foundation, Inc.
909 NE Loop 410, Suite 500, San Antonio, Texas 78209
1-800-457-0777
www.warmsprings.org

Library of Congress Number: 97-60337
ISBN: 0-9656887-0-4

Editorial material compiled and written by Janelle L. Fischer

Edited, Designed and Manufactured by
Favorite Recipes® Press
P.O. Box 305142, Nashville, Tennessee 37230
1-800-358-0560

Manufactured in the United States of America
First Printing: 1997 7,500

About The Cover:

The original warm springs, discovered during oil exploration in the early 1900s, became the focal point of physical rehabilitation in Texas after the founding of the first Warm Springs Rehabilitation Hospital in 1937.

Foreword

As a former Warm Springs patient, I was honored to be asked to contribute to *Recipes for Success*, a special cookbook created to celebrate Warm Springs' 60-year history of providing rehabilitation services to Texans of all ages. The title *Recipes for Success* is quite fitting for an organization that seems to know the secret to providing a positive, healing impact on the lives of thousands. It was this "can do" attitude that helped me when, at age fifteen, I was stricken with polio.

I am proud to say I was one of Warm Springs' earliest patients. I was admitted to Gonzales Warm Springs Rehabilitation Hospital in September 1945 for treatment of a severe case of polio, which affected both my arms and legs. I arrived there after a month in an iron lung breathing machine in a San Antonio hospital. Still a teenager, I was worried about what my future would hold. In those days, a person with physical disabilities didn't really have much of a future. Despite what some doctors and others said at the time, I refused to accept my current condition. I was determined to do the very best with whatever abilities I might be able to regain.

Warm Springs' first physical therapist, Loraine Millican, specialized in the Sister Kenny Method for the treatment of polio. Every day she and the nurses would soak wool Pullman Railroad blankets in boiling water and wrap them around our stiff, aching limbs. We also received therapies in the indoor pool, filled with water from the original warm springs located on the hospital grounds. I arrived almost unable to move. I was discharged ten months later using only a cane for support.

When I look back today on my time as a patient at Warm Springs, I am still motivated by the loving, caring, and positive attitude of the staff. That, in addition to my own determination, has helped energize me throughout my whole career. It was what drew me to the field of medicine when people thought I shouldn't be allowed to attend medical school as a post-polio victim due to my physical limitations. It was what made me deeply concerned for the needs and fears of my own patients. It was what made me aware of the importance of approaching disability with creative energy and optimism.

What started as the state's first rehabilitation hospital has now grown into the Warm Springs Rehabilitation System, a comprehensive organization of inpatient and outpatient centers located across the state. But that original Warm Springs spirit, first established in 1937, is still strongly alive today. I believe my "recipes for success" in my medical career are based on what I learned as a patient: equal parts of inspiration and loving care make all the difference in the world.

Harold N. Cooper, M.D.

Harold N. Cooper, M.D.
San Antonio, Texas

Preface

Welcome to *Recipes for Success*, a cookbook celebrating the 60-year history of the Warm Springs Rehabilitation System, founded in 1937 near Gonzales, Texas. The purpose of this book is to share with you some of the many success stories that make up our history. Inside you will find profiles on some of our special programs, quotes from many of our successful former patients, tips from our therapists on adapted cooking techniques, and favorite recipes from all over Texas.

As a not-for-profit organization, Warm Springs has remained dedicated to providing greater access to services for the reduction and prevention of disability. Through innovative rehabilitation, education, and community outreach programs, we have set a standard for comprehensive inpatient and outpatient rehabilitation services in the state of Texas. One of our most important special community outreach programs is Warm Springs Wheelchair Sports. Founded in 1989, it provides hundreds of challenged athletes from Texas and the nation with a myriad of organized competitive and recreational opportunities.

The proceeds from this cookbook are committed to the expansion of our Wheelchair Sports Program. In assessing the needs of those with physical disabilities, the demand for improved quality of life remains at the top of the list. Through programs such as Wheelchair Sports, people with physical disabilities can achieve active and healthy lifestyles—the types of lifestyles we all need to reach our true potential.

Throughout its history, Warm Springs has been blessed with thousands of supporters from across the state and the nation. Thank you for purchasing our cookbook or for receiving it with open arms. The sales of this book will help us make an even greater impact on the lives of children and adults with special needs.

With warm regards,

Kay Peck

Kay E. Peck
President/CEO
Warm Springs
Rehabilitation Foundation

Contents

History of Warm Springs	6
History of Warm Springs Wheelchair Sports	8
Contributors	10
Appetizers	12
Success Is Beginning —	
Warm Springs Education and Injury Prevention	
Soups & Salads	22
Success Is Relationships —	
Warm Springs Animal-Assisted Therapy Program	
Main Dishes	42
Success Is Healing —	
Physical Medicine and Rehabilitation Services	
Side Dishes & Breads	80
Success Is Independence —	
Warm Springs Long-Term Supported Living	
Desserts	104
Success Is Opportunity —	
Warm Springs Resource Center	
About the Artist — Beth Eidelberg	154
Index	156

History of Warm Springs

The original warm springs, the historical heart of the first Warm Springs Rehabilitation Hospital, were discovered quite by accident by an oil exploration team in 1909. Copies of original drilling logs say that drilling along the San Marcos River (in Palmetto State Park near Gonzales, Texas) was first done in 1907 by Brown Oil Company. Financial problems caused the prospecting to be taken over by the Heywood Oil Company of Beaumont. Heywood abandoned its first hole after reaching 1,500 feet.

The Producers Oil Company of Houston accepted the challenge and started drilling with a 2.5-inch pipe. In September 1909, the crew hit two feet of sandy limestone, which quickly became "mean rock." After coring five feet and ruining three drills, workers sought the help of Howard R. Hughes, inventor of the cone rock bit. Crews were then able to drill two more feet before hitting water sand. On October 9, 1909, the initial artesian flow was discovered at 98.5 degrees and 100 gallons per minute.

The Producers Oil Company then abandoned the site and relocated operations to the west side of the San Marcos River. In February 1910, an analysis of the water was done, and experts concluded at the time that its mineral-rich composition would make it of high medicinal value to those who might bathe in it.

The well stood dormant for nearly 30 years until the eight Warm Springs founders decided to establish a rehabilitation center at the site during the outbreak of the polio epidemic.

Some 60 years ago, the following Texans incorporated themselves to form the Gonzales Warm Springs Foundation for Crippled Children: Ross Boothe, Glen Burgess, S. H. Burchard, Joseph Grant, M. S. Spooner, Dr. George Holmes, Henry Reese III, and Frank Boehm. Construction of the first hospital unit, housing 16 patients, was completed in 1939, and the natural springs bubbled endlessly from the large stone fountain in front of the complex. According to the first Warm Springs physical therapist, Loraine Millican now of Corpus Christi, the water was pumped in a small pool located at the front of the hospital building. There, children could reap its therapeutic benefits during scheduled sessions of prescribed physical exercise.

The location of the hospital so near the springs would also help bring a revolutionary polio treatment technique to Texas in the early 1940s. The technique, called the Kenny Method after Sister Elizabeth Kenny of the University of Minnesota, promoted the use of hot packs and pool therapy instead of friction massage of the painful muscles. During this period, Millican was the first Texas therapist to travel north to attend training in the new treatment.

Several years later, the springs were also tapped to fill a large outdoor pool on the campus, which eventually would include several large Spanish-style buildings.

W. B. Sharp, president of the Producers Oil Company of Houston, proudly displays the artesian springs his company drilled in 1909 with the help of a special cone rock bit invented by Howard R. Hughes. The 106-degree springs, discovered at a depth of 1,550 feet, flowed at 9,000 gallons per hour and Warm Springs became their namesake.

During World War II, through financial and supply shortages, leaders of the organization continued to push for its success. Since its founding in 1937, local supporters and active former patients have hosted fund-raisers of all kinds. By 1946, Warm Springs leaders had collected more than $400,000 from across the state to erect additional buildings on the Gonzales campus. In the late 1940s, the Foundation's efforts would take off and the cities of Fort Worth, Houston, Beaumont, and others would help finance the construction of several large buildings worth nearly a half million dollars. Patients would continue to pour in from across the state until the Salk vaccine ended the epidemic. Warm Springs, however, adapted to the changing need for rehabilitative services and began to focus on treatment of people with catastrophic injuries in addition to chronic disease.

In 1989, Warm Springs would expand for the first time. Warm Springs Rehabilitation Hospital–San Antonio (now Warm Springs+Baptist Rehabilitation Hospital following a 1993 affiliation agreement with Baptist Health System) opened its doors to both inpatients and outpatients. Shortly thereafter, the system founded the Warm Springs Wheelchair Sports Program.

In 1992, Warm Springs added a third inpatient facility in Corpus Christi. Since the early 1990s, Warm Springs has continued its growth to provide comprehensive physical medicine and rehabilitation services. Warm Springs outpatient rehabilitation centers and services are now available in cities such as Lubbock, Falfurrias, Corpus Christi, McAllen, San Benito, San Antonio, Pearsall, and New Braunfels.

Warm Springs Rehabilitation System now serves more than 1,900 inpatients and provides for more than 60,000 outpatient visits per year. Most recently, the system and the original warm springs were the subject of a 1995 episode of "The Eyes of Texas" produced by Ron Stone Films of Houston.

History of Warm Springs Wheelchair Sports

In 1989, Warm Springs began to extend its mission to improve quality of life for people with disabilities through a new and unique program: Wheelchair Sports. Sponsored by the Warm Springs Rehabilitation Foundation, the program has grown from one participant to a widely publicized and professionally organized comprehensive recreational and competitive sports program for those with mobility impairments.

"Our goal back then is the same as it is now," says Warm Springs Wheelchair Sports founder and certified therapeutic recreation specialist Pam Wimberley. "The program strives to provide a variety of enjoyable activities for people to explore their potential. But Wheelchair Sports is more than just special opportunities. It's about helping give meaning back to peoples' lives after a devastating injury or illness."

As an active, visible arm of the Warm Springs mission, Wheelchair Sports has evolved from just a few sports opportunities to a comprehensive list of recreational and competitive activities. They include: basketball, bowling, camping, canoeing, handcrank cycling, dancing, fishing, football, horseback riding, kayaking, martial arts, nature hiking, power soccer, quad rugby, racquetball, road racing, roller hockey, scuba diving, snowskiing, swimming, team handball, table tennis, track and field, tennis, waterskiing, and wellness/fitness programming. The program currently serves an estimated 500 athletes, both former patients and community residents.

"Many of our participants have been very successful at higher levels of competition," says Ross Davis, Wheelchair Sports coordinator. "We've sent kids to Junior Nationals in track and field, and we've also had individuals excel and qualify for the International Paralympic Games."

Davis, 1996 Paralympic gold and bronze medal winner in the 100m and 400m sprints respectively, also won four silver medals in the 1992 Paralympics. Other Paralympic qualifiers and Warm Springs Wheelchair Sports participants include Gabe Diaz de Leon (field events) and Joby Falk (quad rugby).

"One of the most rewarding things I can do is to open up the world of sports and competition to a child," Davis says. "Once they see what they can do, they begin to overcome those feelings of what they can't do."

In 1996, the Warm Springs Wheelchair Sports Program sponsored its first official event to recognize the motivation and special achievements of its participants. The annual Wheelchair Sports Banquet was hosted by the Foundation at Warm Springs+ Baptist Rehabilitation Hospital in San Antonio. Warm Springs President/CEO Kay Peck presented plaques to the night's honorees: the Louis Vance Family—Family of the Year; Doug Schwirtz—Junior Athlete of the Year; Larry Quintero—Adult Athlete of the Year; and Josh Cox—Volunteer of the Year.

Doug Schwirtz hits the wake at the ALLCANSKI adapted waterski event co-hosted each fall by Warm Springs Wheelchair Sports and Sea World of Texas.

In January 1997, the Wheelchair Sports Program hosted its second banquet. The night's honorees included: the David McAllister Family—Family of the Year; David Scott Roberts—Junior Athlete of the Year; Gilbert Garcia—Adult Athlete of the Year; and Floyd Czaja—Volunteer of the Year.

"Warm Springs Wheelchair Sports has grown extensively in its eight years," Davis says. "And we're advocating for an even greater community involvement to assist us in expanding current programming to meet the needs of people with disabilities in our area and in other Texas communities."

Wheelchair Sports brochures, newsletters, and videotapes are available upon request. For more information on the program's activities or volunteer opportunities, call (210) 616-0100, Texas toll-free 1-800-741-6321, or contact us at Internet address www.warmsprings.org. For more information on sponsorship/gifts/contributions, call 1-800-457-0777.

Contributors

Donald Allen
Beverly Anderson
Jean Anderson
Onie Baker
Jane Barnes
Jennifer Barnes
Jean Beach
Shirley Becker
Gayle Bell
Barbara Blair
Jenny Blair
Emma Blakeway
Dewanda Blenden
Marguerite H. Bohne
Emi Bozka
Ophelia Brown
Nathaniel R. Bruce
Bonnie Buchholtz
Carolyn Buschfort
Becki Carley
Katherine Carlson
Louella Carr
Jean Peck Carroll
Wanda Casey
Verna Chandler
Rita R. Charles
Shawna Chumchal
Debra Clark
Lisa Clark
Dean Coldeway
Mark Collins

Myrtle Colwell
Nathan Cowart
Barbara J. Cox
Verna Cunningham
Linda Lee Davis
Vicki Davis
Lorine M. Dierschke
Violet Dietze
Jill Dodds
Ann Driver
Bettie Driver
Carolyn Driver
Hazel Duncan
Ruby Engelke
Pat Eska
Emily Ess
Phyllis Ewers
Margaret Favor
Vicki Fisher
Donna R. Flores
Michelle Flores
Mollie Gates
Lillian Gohlke
Vernie Gomez
Dolores Gonzalez
Frances Goodwin
Garland Goodwin
Virginia Grant
Leslie Guess
Steve Hahn
Isabelle Hall

Susan Hall
Charlene Hanz
Karen Hayden
Mildred Hays
Bobbie J. Hetrick
Tammy Hillman
Reta Hines
Margarita Hinojosa
Shirley Hodges
Fredda Humphries
Nancy Hunt
Vanessa Ireland
Elvera Jaks
Patty Janzen
Mildred Jarvis
Marion M. Jeffers
Erin Johnson
Josephine Johnson
Cathy L. Jones
Kathy Jurek
Deanne Kindred
Jossie Krametbauer
Bob Kuhn
Sharon Kuhn
Marian Kuntschik
Connie Kuykendoll
Lindee Larsen
Gladys Lindemann
Shirley L. Loban
Michael Mahaffey
Jennifer Malatek

Cecilia N. Maresh
Louisa Mata
Arla May
Susan Mayfield
Cecile McAllister
Arthur B. McKinney
Theresa Meitzen
Conan Gay Meyer
Abbi Michelson
Emma G. Miller
Marcia Moore
Jennie M. Munk
Evelyn Mutschler
Charles E. Nickles
Vicki Odom
Dottie Oliver
Scarlett O'Neill
Marsha Orr
Barbara Otto
Carla Patterson
Linda Patteson
James Peck
Jane Peck
Kay Peck
Patricia Perryman
Barbara and Tommy Phillips
Ida Helen Pieper
Jack Pirson
Dorothy Ploeger
Adele Pouncey
Addie M. Pratt

Marilyn Price
Gloria Ramirez
Edith Reece
Donna Reichel
Melinda Roberts
Isaac L. Robinson
Verna Mae Rodgers
Cleta Mae Roeber
Betty J. Rogers
Jerilynn Rohrbacher
Floy Ross
Kermit and Corinne Rudloff
Frank Sancho
Betty Schmidt
Heidi Schoenfeld
Kitty Schustereit
Lynette Sierer
Kimberly Simmons
Jane Snow
Christine Sommers
Lula M. Spears
Catherine Spruce
Vannie Starr
Gee Gee Steves
Dorothy Stoeltje
Diane Stoffer
Ava Street
Bonnie Street
Janie Tew
Lou Tew
Valerie Tew

Suesy Thomas
Skipper Truitt
Mary Tupacz
Deana Voges
Barbara H. Ward
Candi Ward
Jo Ann Wigodsky
Carolyn Williams
Dorothy Williamson
Margie Williamson
David A. Wilson
Marguerite Wilson
Pam Wimberley
Glenna Winegeart
Carol Winscott
Helen G Worsham
Devin Zakrzewski
Susan Zakrzewski
Edwin E. Zapalac
Linda Zealy
Kenneth Zimmern

Success Is Beginning — Warm Springs Education and Injury Prevention

The mission of Warm Springs Rehabilitation System includes a strong emphasis on education and injury prevention. In addition to providing research, advocacy, and compassionate care, Warm Springs is committed to reducing the occurrence of debilitating injury and disease.

Today, Warm Springs takes this commitment to all of its locations. In San Antonio, Gonzales, and Corpus Christi, for example, Warm Springs therapists, health education coordinators, and former patients present the "Play It Safe" Spinal Cord and Head Injury Prevention Program. Elementary schoolchildren from these cities and surrounding school districts hear testimonials from former patients such as Victoria resident Mickey Lange, survivor of a serious spinal cord injury.

Lange, who spent many weeks in intense therapy at Gonzales Warm Springs, overcame the paralysis he suffered after a near-deadly dive into Coletto Creek in 1993. Despite doctors' prognoses that he'd never walk again, Lange left Warm Springs under his own power, assisted only by a pair of special crutches. He now walks with no assistance and has returned to work.

Following the presentations, speakers host drawings for bicycle helmets. In addition, the student participants receive reflective safety stickers to mount on their own helmets or bicycles.

For more information on the Warm Springs Education and Injury Prevention Program, call 1-800-741-6321.

Appetizers

Warm Springs therapist Rita Ramos
helps grade schoolers from
Corpus Christi learn ways to
"Play it Safe" during their summer
vacation by preventing spinal cord
and head injuries.

Artichoke Dip

1 (15-ounce) can artichoke hearts, drained, chopped
1 cup mayonnaise
1 cup grated Parmesan cheese
1 tablespoon paprika

Combine the artichokes, mayonnaise and cheese in a bowl and mix well. Spoon into a 1-quart baking dish. Sprinkle with the paprika. Bake at 400 degrees for 40 minutes. Serve warm with wheat crackers.
  Makes 15 to 20 servings.

Candi Ward
Kingsville, Texas

Pancho Villa's Dip

2 cups sour cream
1 (4-ounce) can chopped green chiles
1½ (15-ounce) cans spicy refried beans
4 avocados, mashed
4 tomatoes, chopped
1 (4-ounce) can chopped ripe olives, drained
8 ounces Longhorn or Cheddar cheese, shredded

Combine the sour cream and chiles in a bowl and mix well. Spread the refried beans on a 12-inch plate. Layer the sour cream mixture, avocados, tomatoes and olives in the order listed over the beans. Sprinkle with the cheese. Serve with tortilla chips. May add a layer of browned ground beef; may add a layer of shredded lettuce under or over the beans.
  Makes 18 to 20 servings.

Barbara Otto
Shiner, Texas

Hot and Spicy Shrimp Dip

1   (15-ounce) can artichoke hearts, drained
8   ounces small cooked peeled shrimp
½   cup mayonnaise
½   cup hot sauce
¼   cup grated Romano cheese
3   ounces cream cheese, softened

Combine the artichoke hearts, shrimp, mayonnaise, hot sauce, Romano cheese and cream cheese in a bowl and mix well. Spoon into a greased baking dish. Bake at 350 degrees for 20 minutes. Serve with assorted party crackers.

Makes 12 to 15 servings.

Cecile McAllister
San Antonio, Texas

Libby's Dip

8   ounces cream cheese, softened
1   (15-ounce) can artichoke hearts
1   cup mayonnaise
1   cup sour cream
1   envelope Italian salad dressing mix

Combine the cream cheese, artichokes, mayonnaise, sour cream and dressing mix in a food processor container. Process until mixed. Spoon into a serving bowl. Chill, covered, until serving time. Serve with corn chips. Do not use mayonnaise-type salad dressing in this recipe.

Makes 10 to 15 servings.

Marion M. Jeffers
San Antonio, Texas

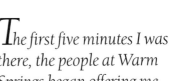

The first five minutes I was there, the people at Warm Springs began offering me hope. They were 100 percent professional, from the doctors to the housekeepers. Yet they still made all the patients feel special. I went there with the attitude that these people could help me. I soon began to see that these people would show me how I could help myself.

J. L. "Doc" Laird, former Guillain-Barre Syndrome patient, Corpus Christi, Texas

Mexican Layered Dip

1	can bean dip
1	(15-ounce) can refried beans
8	ounces cream cheese, softened
2	tablespoons mayonnaise
1	tablespoon picante sauce
1	cup (or more) guacamole
8	ounces Cheddar cheese, shredded
8	ounces Monterey Jack cheese, shredded
1	cup chopped fresh tomatoes
1	cup chopped green onions with tops
1	(4-ounce) can sliced black olives, drained

Combine the bean dip and refried beans in a bowl and mix well. Spread on a large serving platter. Combine the cream cheese, mayonnaise and picante sauce in a bowl and mix well. Spread over the prepared layer. Top with the guacamole. Sprinkle with the Cheddar cheese, Monterey Jack cheese, tomatoes, green onions and olives in the order listed. Serve with corn chips.

Makes 15 to 20 servings.

Ruby Engelke
Seguin, Texas

Tip: *Simplify all details. Example: Store items used most often in the most accessible cupboards and drawers, and pre-position similar equipment and supplies together—baking needs, cleaning needs, etc.*

Cheese Balls

16	ounces cream cheese, softened
¼	cup chopped olives
¼	cup minced onion
2	tablespoons minced fresh parsley
2	tablespoons mayonnaise
1	tablespoon Worcestershire sauce
⅛	teaspoon Tabasco sauce
	Dried or chipped beef

Combine the cream cheese, olives, onion, parsley, mayonnaise, Worcestershire sauce and Tabasco sauce in a bowl and mix well. Chill, covered, for 2 hours. Shape into 1-inch balls. Cut the beef with kitchen scissors. Wrap the beef around each cheese ball. Arrange on a serving platter. Makes 20 to 25 servings.

Jane Peck
El Paso, Texas

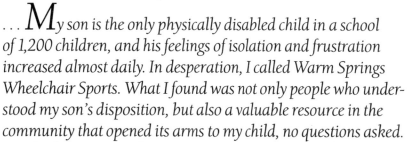

...*My son is the only physically disabled child in a school of 1,200 children, and his feelings of isolation and frustration increased almost daily. In desperation, I called Warm Springs Wheelchair Sports. What I found was not only people who understood my son's disposition, but also a valuable resource in the community that opened its arms to my child, no questions asked.*

Wheelchair Sports has presented opportunities that we did not even know existed, and the metamorphosis in my son has been nothing short of amazing! It's clear that the goals he is now striving for bring him great happiness. His teacher asked what we had done for him as his attitude and behavior in school had markedly improved.

Thank you for supporting such an incredible asset to our community! It has created a new little athlete and given him a hopeful outlook. A need has been met in my child that would not have been possible without Warm Springs Wheelchair Sports....

Theresa Kenworthy, mother of Wheelchair Sports participant,
San Antonio, Texas

Shrimp Mold

1 envelope unflavored gelatin
¼ cup cold water
1 (10-ounce) can tomato soup
1 cup mayonnaise
8 ounces cream cheese, softened
2 pounds shrimp, cooked, peeled, deveined, chopped
¾ cup finely chopped celery
¼ cup finely chopped onion
½ teaspoon salt
½ teaspoon pepper

Dissolve the gelatin in the water in a bowl and mix well. Whisk in the tomato soup. Process the gelatin mixture, mayonnaise and cream cheese in a blender or food processor until smooth. Fold in the shrimp, celery and onion. Season with the salt and pepper. Spoon into a greased 8-cup mold. Chill until set. Invert onto a serving platter. Serve with assorted party crackers.

Makes 15 to 20 servings.

Bettie Driver
Atlanta, Georgia

Curried Spinach and Apple Spread

2 (10-ounce) packages frozen chopped spinach, thawed
¾ cup mayonnaise
  Curry powder to taste
1 large unpeeled apple, finely chopped
¾ cup chutney
¾ cup chopped peanuts

Squeeze the moisture from the spinach. Combine the spinach, mayonnaise and curry powder in a bowl and mix well. Stir in the apple, chutney and peanuts. Chill, covered, until serving time. Serve with assorted party crackers or fresh vegetables.

Makes 15 to 20 servings.

Jane Snow
El Paso, Texas

Cheese Rings

16 ounces extra-sharp Cheddar cheese, shredded
3 cups flour
1 cup margarine, softened
¼ cup olive oil
1½ teaspoons cayenne
1 teaspoon salt

Combine the cheese, flour, margarine, olive oil, cayenne and salt in a food processor container. Process until the mixture forms a ball. Spoon into a cookie press. Pipe into 1½-inch circles on a baking sheet sprayed with nonstick cooking spray. Bake at 350 degrees for 18 minutes or until the edges are light brown. Remove to a wire rack to cool.

Makes 30 servings.

Linda Zealy
Victoria, Texas

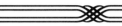

Today, more than a year after the beginning of my very serious illness, I feel really well and am back at my old activities: gardening, walking, and housework, with no cane. I have not been dancing yet but plan to do that in January at the Scottish Society Ball.

Estelle Pennycuick, former patient, San Antonio, Texas

Hot Crab Meat Ramekins

1 1/3	cups sliced mushrooms
1/4	cup minced onion
1/2	cup melted butter
1	pound lump crab meat
1	cup bread crumbs
1	teaspoon salt
1/2	teaspoon thyme
1/4	teaspoon pepper
2	cups light cream
2	egg yolks, lightly beaten
3/4	cup buttered bread crumbs
	Paprika to taste

Sauté the mushrooms and onion in the butter in a skillet; reduce heat. Simmer for 5 to 7 minutes, stirring frequently. Stir in the crab meat, bread crumbs, salt, thyme and pepper. Add a mixture of the light cream and egg yolks, mixing well. Spoon into buttered ramekins or baking shells or a buttered 2-quart baking dish. Sprinkle with the bread crumbs and paprika. Bake at 375 degrees for 20 to 25 minutes or until bubbly.

Makes 8 to 10 servings.

Barbara H. Ward
Austin, Texas

Armadillo Eggs

- 8 ounces Monterey Jack cheese, shredded
- 8 ounces bulk hot sausage, crumbled
- 1½ cups buttermilk baking mix
  Canned whole jalapeños
- 8 ounces Monterey Jack cheese, cut into strips
- 1 package Pork Shake'n Bake
  Eggs, lightly beaten

Combine 8 ounces shredded cheese and sausage in a bowl and mix well. Add the baking mix ½ cup at a time, mixing well after each addition to form a stiff dough. Knead several times. Slice the jalapeños lengthwise into halves; discard the seeds. Stuff each half with a cheese strip; pinch to enclose the cheese. Shape a small amount of the sausage mixture into a ball; pat to flatten. Place a stuffed jalapeño in the center; wrap to seal. Roll into the shape of an egg. Coat with Shake'n Bake; dip in eggs. Roll in Shake'n Bake again. Arrange the jalapeños on a baking sheet. Repeat the process with the remaining sausage mixture and stuffed jalapeños. Bake at 300 to 350 degrees for 20 to 25 minutes or until light brown.

Makes variable servings.

Lynette Sierer
Marion, Texas

Pinwheels

Flour tortillas
Cream cheese, softened
Finely chopped green onions
Finely chopped olives
Finely chopped cooked ham
Finely chopped seeded jalapeños (optional)

Spread the tortillas with cream cheese; sprinkle with the green onions, olives, ham and jalapeños. Roll to enclose the filling. Wrap tightly in plastic wrap. Chill until serving time. Cut into 1/2-inch slices.

Makes variable servings.

Becki Carley
Seguin, Texas

Melinda Roberts
San Antonio, Texas

EZ Party Pecans

1/2 cup margarine
4 1/2 tablespoons Worcestershire sauce
2 to 3 teaspoons seasoned salt, or to taste
2 pounds pecan halves

Microwave the margarine in a microwave-safe dish until melted. Stir in the Worcestershire sauce and seasoned salt. Add the pecans, stirring to coat. Spread on a baking sheet. Bake at 250 degrees for 1 hour, stirring every 15 minutes. Spread on paper towels to cool.

Makes 16 to 20 servings.

Edwin E. Zapalac
Flatonia, Texas

Success Is Relationships — Warm Springs Animal-Assisted Therapy Program

Since 1988, Warm Springs has provided the therapeutic application of animals in the rehabilitation process of its patients. Across the street from Gonzales Warm Springs Rehabilitation Hospital, few might notice the small fenced arena gently shaded by massive oak trees. But two days a week, horses arrive at the serene setting to offer patients the restorative interaction only such sturdy and graceful creatures can provide.

In San Antonio, at Warm Springs+ Baptist Rehabilitation Hospital, it's the soft sound of a dog's paws that brings a smile and an extra boost of motivation to patients.

Warm Springs has provided therapeutic horseback riding for nine years through a special relationship with A.W.A.R.E. (Always Wanted A Riding Experience), a not-for-profit accredited program operating near San Marcos. Kerstin Fosdick, Warm Springs physical therapist and riding program coordinator, says the activity is known as one of the most modern and progressive forms of therapy and recreation. Through working with specially trained staff and therapists, patients can increase muscle strength and relaxation; improve posture, balance, and coordination; and increase joint mobility. In addition to physical benefits, riding can also help improve concentration, develop self- and body-awareness, and build self-confidence.

Fosdick says the natural gait of the horse provides simultaneous movement in three planes—up and down, fore and aft, and side to side. This requires patients to accommodate the movements, through automatic reactions, which helps them relearn the sensory imprint of their own walking movements.

Since 1993, the Animal-Assisted Therapy Program at Warm Springs+Baptist Rehabilitation Hospital has provided therapeutic application of the natural healing bond between animals and humans. Warm Springs therapists work with the dogs as catalysts to help patients meet physiological, physical, psychological, speech/language, and other rehabilitation goals. The AAT program and the hospital's animal visitation program are made possible through a unique partnership between Warm Springs and San Antonio-area community volunteers.

All dogs used in the program must meet special temperament and grooming requirements. Delta San Antonio provides special training and testing programs for these Pet Partners. The AAT program provides therapy to approximately 140 patients per year for an average of 120 volunteer hours donated to the program annually (not counting special training, testing, and grooming required by dog owners/handlers in order to participate in the program).

For more information on therapeutic horseback riding, call (210) 672-6592. For more information on the use of dogs in animal-assisted therapy, call (210) 616-0100.

Soups & Salads

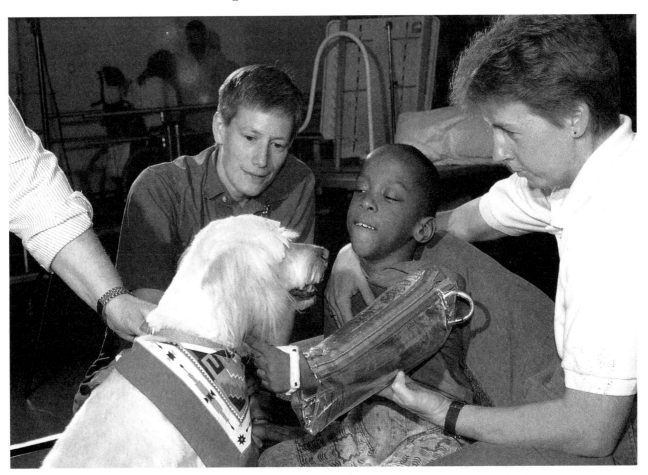

Warm Springs physical therapists Liz Shively and Bev MacGray encourage Richard Adams to improve his strength and coordination by interacting with Sam, owned by Delores Zepeda, San Antonio, Texas.

Borsch

1	cup dried navy beans
2½	pounds lean beef
8	ounces slab bacon
10	cups cold water
1	carrot
1	rib celery
1	large red onion
8	whole peppercorns
2	cloves of garlic
2	tablespoons dried parsley
1	teaspoon salt (optional)
1	bay leaf
8	beets
2	small beets, grated
2	cups shredded green cabbage
2	large leeks, sliced
3	medium potatoes, cut into eighths
1	(29-ounce can) tomatoes
¼	cup sugar
3	tablespoons red wine vinegar
1	tablespoon tomato paste
1	pound kielbasa, sliced (optional)
2	tablespoons flour
1	tablespoon melted butter
½	cup sour cream (optional)

Sort and rinse the beans. Combine the beans with enough water to cover in a stockpot. Soak for 8 to 10 hours. Cook until tender, stirring occasionally; drain. Bring the beef, bacon and 10 cups cold water to a boil in a stockpot; skim. Add the carrot, celery, onion, peppercorns, garlic, parsley, salt and bay leaf and mix well. Simmer, covered, for 1½ hours, stirring occasionally. Cook 8 beets in boiling water in a saucepan for 45 minutes or until tender; drain. Let stand until cool. Peel and cut each beet into eighths. Combine 2 grated beets with enough water to cover in a bowl. Remove the beef and bacon from the soup to a platter. Strain the soup into another stockpot, discarding the vegetables, peppercorns, garlic and bay leaf. Add the beef, bacon, cooked beets, cabbage, leeks, potatoes, tomatoes, sugar, wine vinegar and tomato paste. Bring to a boil; reduce heat. Simmer for 45 minutes, stirring occasionally. Stir in the kielbasa and beans.

Simmer for 20 minutes longer, stirring occasionally. Stir in a mixture of the flour and butter. Cook until slightly thickened, stirring frequently. Strain the grated beets, reserving the liquid and discarding the beets. Add the reserved liquid to the soup and mix well. Cook just until heated through. May add additional sugar or vinegar for a sweeter or more sour flavor. Remove the beef and bacon with a slotted spoon to a platter; slice. Arrange the sliced beef and bacon in soup bowls. Pour the hot soup over the meat. Top each serving with a dollop of sour cream.

Makes 10 servings.

Deana Voges
San Antonio, Texas

Tess worked in the Animal-Assisted Therapy Program even though she was wearing a splint on her leg from making a bad landing in a training exercise. When Tess came into Warm Springs to work with patients, a lady who had had knee surgery and had her leg in a splint said, "Oh sweetie, I know just how you feel!"

Nancy Dragotta, Warm Springs+ Baptist Rehabilitation Hospital education coordinator and Animal-Assisted Therapy Program co-director, commenting on her dog Tess, San Antonio, Texas

Canadian Cheese Soup

1/2	cup finely chopped onion
1/2	cup finely chopped carrot
1/2	cup finely chopped celery
1/4	cup butter
1/4	cup flour
1 1/2	tablespoons cornstarch
4	cups chicken stock
4	cups milk
1	cup shredded Cheddar cheese
1/8	teaspoon baking soda
	Salt and pepper to taste
1/4	cup finely chopped fresh parsley

Cook the onion, carrot and celery in the butter in a saucepan over low heat until tender, stirring frequently. Stir in the flour and cornstarch. Cook until bubbly, stirring constantly. Add the stock and milk and mix well. Cook until of sauce consistency, stirring constantly. Stir in the cheese and baking soda. Season with salt and pepper. Cook just until the cheese melts, stirring constantly. Stir in the parsley just before serving. Ladle into soup bowls.

Makes 8 to 10 servings.

Ava Street
Abilene, Texas

White Corn Chowder

4	shallots, finely chopped
2	cloves of garlic, minced
3	tablespoons unsalted butter
1	or 2 jalapeños, roasted, peeled, seeded, chopped
3	cups fresh cooked white corn
1	cup chicken stock
	Salt to taste
1½	cups whipping cream
¼	cup chopped fresh cilantro (optional)

Sauté the shallots and garlic in the butter in a saucepan. Add the jalapeños and mix well. Cook for 1 minute. Add the corn and stock. Bring to a boil; reduce heat. Simmer for 5 minutes, stirring occasionally. Process the mixture in a blender until puréed. Return the mixture to the saucepan. Season with salt. Stir in the whipping cream. Cook just until heated through; do not boil. Ladle into soup bowls. Sprinkle with the cilantro. May substitute frozen or canned corn for the fresh corn.

Makes 4 servings.

Ann Driver
Scotsdale, Arizona

Tip: *Use pliers with built-up handles to turn knobs on your oven and other appliances, and to open paper cartons.*

Chilled Clam Soup

2	(10-ounce) cans beef consommé
2	cups sour cream
2	(8-ounce) cans minced clams, drained
2	tablespoons fresh lime juice
1	tablespoon minced chives
1	teaspoon salt
½	teaspoon pepper

Chill the consommé until set. Whisk the sour cream into the consommé in a bowl. Fold in the clams, lime juice, chives, salt and pepper. Chill, covered, until serving time. Spoon into soup bowls.

Makes 8 servings.

Linda Zealy
Victoria, Texas

Hearty Potato Soup

6	medium potatoes, peeled, sliced
6	ribs celery, chopped
2	carrots, chopped
2	quarts water
1	onion, chopped
6	tablespoons butter or margarine
6	tablespoons flour
1	teaspoon salt
½	teaspoon pepper
1½	cups milk

Cook the potatoes, celery and carrots in the water in a saucepan for 20 minutes or until tender. Drain, reserving the liquid and vegetables. Sauté the onion in the butter in the same saucepan until tender. Stir in the flour, salt and pepper. Add the milk gradually, stirring constantly. Cook until thickened, stirring constantly. Add the reserved vegetables and mix gently. Add 1 cup of the reserved liquid or enough to make of the desired consistency and mix gently. Cook just until heated through, stirring constantly. Ladle into soup bowls.

Makes 8 to 10 servings.

Glenna Winegeart
Gonzales, Texas

Slow-Cooker Soup

1   pound ground beef, browned, drained
3   (10-ounce) cans Healthy Request Hearty Minestrone soup
2   (16-ounce) cans ranch-style beans
1   (10-ounce) can diced tomatoes with green chiles

Layer the ground beef, soup, beans and tomatoes in the order listed in a slow-cooker. Cook on low for 8 hours; do not stir. Stir just before ladling into soup bowls.

Makes 8 servings.

Emi Bozka
Shiner, Texas

Mexican Cream Soup

2   medium tomatoes, peeled, seeded, chopped
2   medium red or green bell peppers, chopped
2   tablespoons vegetable oil
1½ cups chicken broth
1   cup chopped mushrooms
1   (12-ounce) can evaporated milk
    Salt and pepper to taste
2   ounces Monterey Jack cheese, shredded
2   ounces Cheddar cheese, shredded

Sauté the tomatoes and bell peppers in a 3-quart saucepan in the oil until tender. Add the broth and mix well. Simmer for 10 minutes, stirring occasionally. Add the mushrooms and mix well. Stir in the evaporated milk, salt and pepper. Cook just until heated through; do not boil. Add the Monterey Jack cheese and Cheddar cheese, stirring until melted. Ladle into soup bowls immediately. May add 1 small can chopped jalapeños with the tomatoes and bell peppers or 1 small can chopped green chiles with the mushrooms.

Makes 4 servings.

Garland O. Goodwin
Columbus, North Carolina

I can't thank them enough for the fantastic job they did. Even others say Warm Springs can accomplish more than many other places. My doctor says I'm a walking miracle.

Ronald Altuna, former brain-injury patient, Victoria, Texas

Taco Soup

2	pounds ground beef
½	cup chopped onion
2	(15-ounce) cans chopped tomatoes
1	(10-ounce) can tomatoes with green chiles
1	(16-ounce) can whole kernel corn (optional)
1	(15-ounce) can ranch-style beans
1	(15-ounce) can pinto beans
1	envelope taco seasoning mix
1	envelope ranch salad dressing mix

Brown the beef with the onion in a skillet, stirring until the ground beef is crumbly; drain. Combine the ground beef mixture, undrained tomatoes, undrained corn, undrained beans, taco seasoning mix and salad dressing mix in a slow cooker and mix well. Simmer for 2 hours or until of the desired consistency, stirring occasionally. Ladle into soup bowls. Serve over tortilla chips if desired. May add 1 drained and rinsed 15-ounce can of hominy. May freeze for future use.

Makes 12 to 15 servings.

Gladys Lindemann
Cost, Texas

Linda Patteson
Nixon, Texas

Melinda Roberts
San Antonio, Texas

Sopa de Chayote

- ½ onion, chopped
- 2 teaspoons olive oil
- 2 cloves of garlic, minced
- 3 chayotes, peeled, chopped
- 4 cups stock
- ½ cup white wine
- 2 tablespoons minced fresh dillweed
-   Salt and freshly ground pepper to taste
- ½ cup sour cream

Sauté the onion in the olive oil in a stockpot over medium-high heat until tender. Stir in the garlic. Sauté for 1 minute. Add the chayotes, stock, white wine and 1 tablespoon of the dillweed. Bring to a boil; reduce heat. Simmer, covered, for 25 minutes or until the chayotes are tender, stirring occasionally. Process the mixture in a blender until puréed. Season with salt and pepper. Ladle into soup bowls. Top each serving with a dollop of sour cream; sprinkle with the remaining 1 tablespoon dillweed.
  Makes 6 servings.

Jennifer Barnes
Austin, Texas

Tip: *Sit while washing dishes, peeling vegetables, etc.*

Apricot Pineapple Salad

1	(8-ounce) can crushed pineapple
1	(3-ounce) package apricot gelatin
2	(5-ounce) jars baby food strained apricots
8	ounces cream cheese, softened
¾	cup sugar
9	ounces whipped topping
1	cup chopped pecans

Combine the undrained pineapple and gelatin in a saucepan and mix well. Cook over low heat until the gelatin dissolves, stirring constantly. Stir in the apricots, cream cheese and sugar until mixed; do not beat. Chill, covered, until cool. Fold in the whipped topping and pecans.

Makes 10 servings.

Adele Pouncey
Wrightsboro, Texas

Frosted Salad

1	large can juice-pack crushed pineapple
2	(3-ounce) packages lime gelatin
2	cups boiling water
2	(12-ounce) cans lemon-lime soda
3	small bananas, sliced
1	cup miniature marshmallows
½	cup chopped pecans
½	cup sugar
2	tablespoons flour
1	egg, lightly beaten
2	tablespoons butter
1	cup whipped cream
½	cup shredded American cheese

Drain the pineapple, reserving 1 cup of the juice. Dissolve the gelatin in the boiling water in a bowl and mix well. Stir in the soda. Chill just until set. Fold in the pineapple, bananas, marshmallows and pecans. Pour into a 9x13-inch dish. Chill until set. Combine the sugar and flour in a saucepan and mix well. Stir in the reserved pineapple juice and egg. Cook over low heat until thickened, stirring constantly. Remove from heat. Stir in the butter. Let stand until cool. Chill in the refrigerator. Fold in the whipped cream. Spread over the prepared layer. Sprinkle with the cheese. Chill for 8 to 10 hours.

Makes 12 to 15 servings.

Dewanda Blenden
Lockney, Texas

Mango Salad

3 (3-ounce) packages lemon gelatin
3 cups boiling water
8 ounces cream cheese, softened
1 (32-ounce) can mangos
Juice of 1 lime

Combine the gelatin, boiling water and cream cheese in a bowl and mix well. Process 1/2 of the gelatin mixture, 1/2 of the undrained mangos and 1/2 of the lime juice in a blender until creamy. Spoon into a bowl. Repeat the process with the remaining ingredients. Stir into the gelatin mixture in the bowl. Chill, covered, until set.

Makes 8 to 10 servings.

Lisa Clark
Seattle, Washington

Royal Pear Salad

1 (6-ounce) package raspberry gelatin
1 cup boiling water
2 cups cold water
1 (16-ounce) can whole cranberry sauce
1/2 teaspoon lemon juice
1 (29-ounce) can pear halves, drained, chopped
1/2 cup chopped pecans

Dissolve the gelatin in the boiling water in a bowl and mix well. Stir in the cold water, cranberry sauce and lemon juice. Pour into a shallow 2 1/2- to 3-quart dish. Chill until of the consistency of unbeaten egg whites. Fold in the pears and pecans. Chill until set.

Makes 6 to 8 servings.

Lou Tew
Jonesboro, Louisiana

Waldorf Salad

1   cup plain yogurt
1   tablespoon apple cider vinegar
4   envelopes artificial sweetener
3   Rome apples, chopped
1   cup chopped pecans
2   ribs celery, chopped

Combine the yogurt, vinegar and artificial sweetener in a bowl and mix well. Combine the apples, pecans and celery in a bowl and mix well. Add the yogurt mixture, tossing to coat. Chill, covered, until serving time.
   Makes 8 to 10 servings.

Patricia Perryman
Luling, Texas

Chicken and Carrot Salad

2   cups chopped cooked chicken
1   cup shredded carrots
3/4 cup chopped celery
1/2 cup slivered almonds
2   tablespoons finely chopped onion
     Salt and pepper to taste
1   cup mayonnaise
1   tablespoon fresh lemon juice
     Romaine lettuce

Combine the chicken, carrots, celery, almonds, onion, salt and pepper in a bowl and mix well. Stir in a mixture of the mayonnaise and lemon juice. Chill, covered, in the refrigerator. Spoon onto a lettuce-lined serving platter.
   Makes 4 servings.

A Friend of Warm Springs

We were all crying, including the therapist, because he was saying his numbers. Later he said "mama" and then said "papa."

Mary Lou Balderas, mother of pediatric brain-injury patient, Seguin, Texas

Primavera Salad

1	pound broccoli
1	(12-ounce) package bow tie pasta
	Versatile Vinaigrette
10	ounces fresh spinach, trimmed
1	pound smoked turkey breast, cut into thin strips
1	pint cherry tomatoes, cut into halves
1/2	cup chopped fresh basil
1/4	cup chopped fresh parsley
1/3	cup pine nuts, toasted

Discard the tough ends of the broccoli stalks. Cut the florets and stalks into 1-inch pieces. Cook the broccoli in boiling water to cover in a saucepan for 1 minute; drain. Plunge the broccoli into ice water to stop the cooking process. Drain and pat dry. Chill in the refrigerator. Cook the pasta using package directions. Drain and rinse with cold water; drain. Combine the pasta and Versatile Vinaigrette in a bowl, tossing to coat. Spoon into a sealable plastic bag. Chill for 2 to 10 hours. Combine the broccoli, pasta mixture, spinach, turkey, tomatoes, basil, parsley and pine nuts in a bowl and toss gently.

Makes 8 to 10 servings.

Versatile Vinaigrette

2/3	cup vegetable oil
1/4	cup white wine vinegar
1/4	cup water
1	tablespoon freshly ground pepper
1 1/2	teaspoons salt
1	clove of garlic, crushed

Combine the oil, wine vinegar, water, pepper, salt and garlic in a jar with a tight-fitting lid. Shake to mix.

Helen G. Worsham
San Antonio, Texas

*I*n 1991, Fritz Lynch of Houston was electrocuted in an accident that resulted in the amputation of both legs from the mid-calf down. As a window washer, his physically demanding career could have been over. Instead, after more than ten surgeries and extensive inpatient and outpatient rehabilitation at Gonzales Warm Springs Rehabilitation Hospital, Lynch returned to work. His incredible recovery was also featured by the Houston Chronicle and the Dallas Morning News.

During his stay, he and his wife Deborah were able to keep their sense of humor even in such a trying time. As originally recorded in the Warm Springs Foundation's The Source magazine, Deborah tells of when the orthotist fit her husband for his prostheses. She asked, "Will Fritz be able to dance?" The orthotist answered, "Sure!" "Great," she said, "because he never could before!"

Wild Rice Chicken Salad

1	(6-ounce) package long grain and wild rice
2	chicken breasts, grilled, chopped
1	cup finely chopped green onions
1	cup finely chopped celery
1	cup dried cranberries
¾	cup pine nuts, toasted
⅓	cup Martinique Vinaigrette salad dressing

*C*ook the rice using package directions. Combine the rice, chicken, green onions, celery, cranberries and pine nuts in a bowl and mix well. Add the salad dressing, tossing to mix. Chill, covered, until serving time.

Makes 4 servings.

Cecile McAllister
San Antonio, Texas

Mexican Chef Salad

1   pound ground beef
1   (15-ounce) can kidney beans, drained
¼   teaspoon salt
4   tomatoes, chopped
1   onion, chopped
1   head lettuce, shredded
4   ounces Cheddar cheese, shredded
1   (8-ounce) bottle Thousand Island salad dressing or French salad dressing
2   cups crushed tortilla chips
1   cup chopped fresh cilantro (optional)
    Hot sauce to taste
1   large avocado, sliced
    Sliced tomatoes
    Tortilla chips

Brown the hamburger in a skillet, stirring until crumbly; drain. Stir in the kidney beans and salt. Simmer for 10 minutes, stirring occasionally. Toss 4 chopped tomatoes, onion, lettuce and cheese in a bowl. Add the salad dressing, tossing to coat. Add 2 cups crushed tortilla chips, cilantro and hot sauce and mix gently. Stir in the ground beef mixture. Spoon into a serving bowl. Top with the sliced avocado, sliced tomatoes and tortilla chips. For a moister salad add the bean liquid and bring to a boil before simmering.

Makes 4 servings.

Margarita Hinojosa
Corpus Christi, Texas

Tip: *Use an electric can opener rather than a conventional can opener.*

Broccoli and Cauliflower Salad

1   bunch broccoli, chopped
1   head cauliflower, chopped
1   onion, chopped
2   cups mayonnaise
1   cup sour cream
2   tablespoons vinegar
1/8 teaspoon Worcestershire sauce
1/8 teaspoon hot sauce
    Salt and pepper to taste

Toss the broccoli, cauliflower and onion in a bowl. Combine the mayonnaise, sour cream, vinegar, Worcestershire sauce, hot sauce, salt and pepper in a bowl and mix well. Add to the broccoli mixture, tossing to mix. Chill, covered, for 8 to 10 hours.

Makes 6 to 8 servings.

Jerilynn Rohrbacher
Marion, Texas

Floy Ross
Luling, Texas

E-Z Rice Salad

1   cup rice
2   cups water
1   envelope ranch salad dressing mix
1/2 cup mayonnaise
1/4 cup water
2   tablespoons pickle juice
1/4 cup chopped pickles
2   hard-cooked eggs, chopped
2   tablespoons chopped pimento
1/2 teaspoon pepper
1/4 teaspoon celery salt or celery seeds
     Chopped green onions to taste

Combine the rice and 2 cups water in a saucepan. Bring to a boil; reduce heat. Simmer, covered, for 15 minutes. Combine the rice and salad dressing mix in a bowl and mix well. Stir in a mixture of the mayonnaise, 1/4 cup water and pickle juice. Combine the pickles, eggs, pimento, pepper and celery salt in a bowl and mix well. Stir into the rice mixture. Chill, covered, until serving time. Sprinkle with the green onions.

Makes 6 to 8 servings.

Shirley Hodges
Gonzales, Texas

Black Bean Salad

- 3 cups cooked black beans
- 2 cups French-style green beans
- 1 cup cooked garbanzo beans
- 1 cup cooked adzuki beans or red beans
- 2 onions, sliced
- 2 green bell peppers, sliced
- 2 ribs celery, sliced
- 2 green onions, thinly sliced
- 2 cups vegetable oil
- 1 cup white wine
- ½ cup honey
- 2 cloves of garlic, crushed
- Juice of 1 lemon
- 1 tablespoon parsley
- 1 teaspoon oregano

Combine the black beans, green beans, garbanzo beans, adzuki beans, onions, green peppers, celery and green onions in a bowl and mix gently. Combine the oil, white wine, honey, garlic, lemon juice, parsley and oregano in a bowl and mix well. Add to the bean mixture, tossing to coat. Chill, covered, for 8 to 10 hours.

Makes 12 servings.

Deana Voges
San Antonio, Texas

Tip: *Use a sponge when washing dishes and keep your fingers flat. To squeeze out a sponge, place the sponge on a drain board and press down on it.*

German Slaw

1 medium head green cabbage, finely shredded
3 hard-cooked eggs, grated
¼ cup (rounded) mayonnaise-type salad dressing
2 tablespoons sugar
½ teaspoon salt

Combine the cabbage and eggs in a bowl and mix well. Stir in the salad dressing. Add the sugar and salt and mix well. Chill, covered, for 2 hours or longer.

Makes 6 servings.

Kitty Schustereit
Victoria, Texas

Overnight Vegetable Salad

1 (16-ounce) can tiny green peas, drained
1 (16-ounce) can French-style green beans, drained
1 (11-ounce) can Shoe Peg white corn, drained
1 (4-ounce) can sliced black olives, chopped
1 medium onion, finely chopped
¾ cup finely chopped celery
2 tablespoons chopped pimento
½ cup sugar
¼ cup vegetable oil
¼ cup white vinegar
½ teaspoon salt
½ teaspoon pepper

Combine the green peas, green beans, corn, olives, onion, celery and pimento in a bowl and toss gently. Combine the sugar, oil, vinegar, salt and pepper in a saucepan. Cook until the sugar dissolves, stirring frequently. Pour over the vegetable mixture, tossing to coat. Chill, covered, for 8 to 10 hours, stirring occasionally. May store, covered, in the refrigerator for several days.

Makes 10 to 12 servings.

Charlene Hanz
San Antonio, Texas

Seven-Layer Salad

- 3/4 large head lettuce, shredded
- 1 (8-ounce) can sliced water chestnuts, drained
- 1/2 cup chopped celery
- 1/2 cup chopped green bell pepper
- 1/2 cup chopped onion
- 1 (10-ounce) package frozen green peas, cooked, drained, cooled
- 2 cups mayonnaise
- 2 tablespoons sugar
- 6 ounces Cheddar cheese, shredded
- 8 slices crisp-fried bacon, crumbled

Layer the lettuce, water chestnuts, celery, green pepper, onion and peas in the order listed in a 9x13-inch dish. Spread with the mayonnaise, sealing to the edges. Sprinkle with the sugar, cheese and bacon. Chill, covered with foil, for 24 hours.

Makes 12 servings.

Phyllis Ewers
Ponca City, Oklahoma

Barbara and Tommy Phillips
Victoria, Texas

Tip: *To ensure that a tossed salad made in advance will stay crisp, place an inverted saucer in the bottom of the salad bowl. Excess moisture will collect under the saucer.*

Tomato Vegetable Aspic Salad

2	tablespoons unflavored gelatin
1/2	cup cold water
1	(10-ounce) can tomato soup
6	ounces cream cheese
1/2	cup chopped celery
1/2	cup chopped onion
1/2	cup chopped green bell pepper
1	cup mayonnaise

Soften the gelatin in the cold water and mix well. Bring the soup to a boil in a saucepan. Add the cream cheese. Cook until blended, stirring constantly. Remove from heat. Stir in the gelatin mixture. Cool slightly. Stir in celery, onion, green pepper and mayonnaise. Spoon into a mold. Chill until set.

Makes 4 to 6 servings.

A Friend of Warm Springs

Western Salad Dressing

1	cup salad oil
1/2	cup vinegar
1/2	cup sugar
1/4	cup catsup
1	tablespoon grated onion
1	teaspoon salt
1	teaspoon dry mustard
1	teaspoon celery seeds
1	teaspoon paprika
1	clove of garlic, cut into halves

Combine the salad oil, vinegar, sugar, catsup, onion, salt, dry mustard, celery seeds, paprika and garlic in a jar with a tightfitting lid, shaking to mix. Chill until serving time. Discard the garlic. Pour over assorted salad greens.

Makes 2 cups.

Melinda Roberts
San Antonio, Texas

Working with Wheelchair Sports athletes has greatly motivated the activities of my own life. The participants and their overwhelming determination are truly inspiring.

Floyd Czaja, 1997 Wheelchair Sports Volunteer of the Year, San Antonio, Texas

Success Is Healing — Physical Medicine and Rehabilitation Services

For some 60 years Warm Springs Rehabilitation System has used physical medicine and rehabilitation to add value to the lives of hundreds of children and adults with disabilities resulting from catastrophic injuries and chronic illnesses. Today, the system provides comprehensive inpatient and outpatient services across Texas.

In order to better address the complex needs of patients, the hospitals and outpatient settings of the Warm Springs system moved from a departmental approach to an interdisciplinary team approach to delivering rehabilitation services. In 1990, the system adopted the interdisciplinary model, which requires that rehab team members work together to evaluate the patient, set goals, plan treatment strategies, evaluate progress, and determine a patient's discharge plan. The individual is thus treated as a whole, with problems—and solutions—that cross the boundaries of therapeutic disciplines.

The composition of a Warm Springs interdisciplinary treatment team includes the following:
- Physical medicine and rehabilitation physicians
- Occupational therapists
- Physical therapists
- Psychologists/neuropsychologists
- Certified rehabilitation nurses
- Speech therapists
- Therapeutic recreation specialists
- Social workers/case managers
- Chaplains

In addressing the needs and goals of the patient as a whole person, the team consults the patient, his or her family and significant others, plus the other members of the rehab team itself. Comprehensive rehabilitation programming addresses these general areas of consideration:
- Intellectual abilities and control
- Emotional status and personality involvement
- Psychosocial abilities and family involvement
- Sensory-perceptual and motor skills
- Environmental structure and activities of daily living
- Leisure preferences and recreational skills
- Vocational and educational status
- Expressed wants and needs of the individual and family

Warm Springs' innovative team approach makes it possible to address the rehabilitation needs for children and adults with a wide range of diagnoses such as: spinal cord injury, brain injury, amputation, stroke, orthopedic injury, cardiac conditions, arthritis, post-polio syndrome, sports/work-related injury, chronic pain, osteoporosis, spasticity, and physical deconditioning.

For more information on inpatient or outpatient rehabilitation programs, call 1-800-741-6321, or contact us at Internet address www.warmsprings.org.

Main Dishes

Warm Springs therapists use the buoyant and recreational benefits of a pool to help Agua Dulce patient Chris Rivera recover from a traumatic brain injury. Across the system, Warm Springs emphasizes the unique healing qualities of aquatic therapy for patients with a wide range of diagnoses.

Lemon Herb Pot Roast

- 2 teaspoons lemon pepper
- 1 teaspoon dried basil
- 2 cloves of garlic, crushed
- 1 (3- to 3 1/2-pound) boneless beef chuck roast
- 1 tablespoon olive oil
- 1 cup water
- 1 pound small red potatoes, cut into halves
- 2 cups peeled tiny carrots
- 1 medium onion, cut into 6 wedges
- 2 tablespoons cornstarch
- 2 tablespoons water
- 1/2 teaspoon dried basil

Combine the lemon pepper, 1 teaspoon basil and garlic in a small bowl and mix well. Pat evenly over the surface of the roast. Heat the olive oil in a Dutch oven over medium-high heat until hot. Add the roast. Cook until brown on all sides, turning several times; drain. Add 1 cup water. Simmer, covered, for 2 hours. Add the potatoes, carrots and onion. Simmer, covered, for 40 to 45 minutes or until the vegetables are tender and the roast is done to taste. Remove the vegetables and roast to a heated platter. Skim the fat from the pan drippings. Stir in a mixture of the cornstarch and 2 tablespoons water. Add 1/2 teaspoon basil and mix well. Bring to a boil. Cook until thickened, stirring constantly. Serve with the roast and vegetables.

Makes 6 servings.

Margie Williamson
Ganado, Texas

Dynamite Marinade

1	cup vegetable oil or Italian salad dressing
2	tablespoons grated gingerroot
2	tablespoons soy sauce
1	teaspoon sugar

Combine the oil, gingerroot, soy sauce and sugar in a bowl and mix well. Pour over beef, chicken, pork, shrimp or fish in a shallow dish. Marinate for 30 minutes, turning several times. Grill, broil or bake as desired. May also use as a basting sauce while grilling.

Makes 1 1/4 cups.

Bob Kuhn
Helotes, Texas

Tip: Avoid using a strong grip. If you have trouble holding objects, wrap foam rubber padding around the handles of your knives, pots and pans.

Beef Paprika

1/4	cup shortening
1	(2-pound) boneless beef chuck or round roast, cut into 1-inch cubes
1	cup sliced onion
1	small clove of garlic, minced
1 1/2	cups water
3/4	cup catsup
2	tablespoons Worcestershire sauce
1	tablespoon brown sugar
2	teaspoons salt
2	teaspoons paprika
1/2	teaspoon dry mustard
1/4	cup water
2	tablespoons flour
3	cups hot cooked noodles

Heat the shortening in a skillet until hot. Add the beef, onion and garlic. Cook until the beef is brown on all sides and the onion is tender, stirring constantly. Stir in 1 1/2 cups water, catsup, Worcestershire sauce, brown sugar, salt, paprika and dry mustard. Simmer, covered, for 2 to 2 1/2 hours or until the beef is done to taste. Stir in a mixture of 1/4 cup water and flour gradually. Bring to a boil, stirring constantly. Boil for 1 minute, stirring constantly. Spoon over the hot cooked noodles on a serving platter.

Makes 6 to 8 servings.

Arla May
San Antonio, Texas

Five-Hour Stew

1	(10-ounce) can tomato soup
1	cup water
¼	cup flour
1	(2-pound) boneless beef chuck roast, cut into 1-inch cubes
3	carrots, cut into 1-inch slices
½	cup (1-inch) slices celery
1	large onion, cut into 1-inch pieces
4	medium potatoes, cut into quarters
	Fresh mushrooms (optional)
2	beef bouillon cubes
1	teaspoon oregano
1	teaspoon thyme
1	teaspoon rosemary
1	bay leaf
	Freshly ground pepper to taste

Combine the tomato soup, water and flour in a Dutch oven, stirring until blended. Add the beef, carrots, celery, onion, potatoes, mushrooms, bouillon cubes, oregano, thyme, rosemary, bay leaf and pepper and mix well. Cook at 250 to 275 degrees for 4 to 5 hours or until the beef and vegetables are done to taste. Discard the bay leaf. Serve the stew with corn bread and tossed green salad.

Makes 6 to 8 servings.

Reta Hines
Gonzales, Texas

Tip: Use convenience products such as frozen pre-cut onions, frozen vegetables, and prepared mixes when cooking.

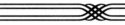

*W*arm Springs actually picked us. The whole thing was a miracle. After meeting us and discovering our situation, one of the acute care hospital employees contacted the preadmission people at Warm Springs. They came to us and said Chris had been accepted as a charity care patient.

*Bobby Rivera, father of former brain-injury patient,
Agua Dulce, Texas*

Black-Eyed Peas and Corn Bread Casserole

1	pound ground beef
1	medium onion, chopped
1	(16-ounce) can black-eyed peas
1	(7-ounce) package corn bread mix
1	cup buttermilk
1	(9-ounce) can cream-style corn
8	ounces Cheddar cheese, shredded
1/2	cup corn oil
2	eggs
2	jalapeños, chopped

*B*rown the ground beef with the onion in a skillet, stirring until the ground beef is crumbly; drain. Combine the black-eyed peas, corn bread mix, buttermilk, corn, cheese, corn oil, eggs and jalapeños in a bowl and mix well. Stir in the ground beef mixture. Spoon into an 8 x 10-inch baking dish sprayed with nonstick cooking spray. Bake the casserole at 350 degrees for 45 minutes.

Makes 20 servings.

*Wanda Casey
Canton, Texas*

Stroganoff Burgers

- 1½ pounds ground beef
- 3 slices bacon, chopped
- ½ cup chopped onion
- 1½ tablespoons flour
- ½ teaspoon salt
- ¼ teaspoon paprika
- 1 (10-ounce) can cream of mushroom soup
- 1 cup sour cream
- ⅛ teaspoon hot sauce or catsup, or to taste
- 8 to 10 buns or kaiser rolls, split, toasted

Brown the ground beef and bacon in a saucepan, stirring until the ground beef is crumbly. Add the onion. Cook just until the onion is tender; drain. Stir in the flour, salt and paprika. Add the soup and mix well. Cook over low heat for 20 minutes, stirring frequently. Stir in the sour cream. Cook just until heated through, stirring occasionally. Stir in the hot sauce just before serving. Serve on the buns. May add 2 tablespoons sauterne or sherry to the mixture. May use reduced-fat soup and nonfat sour cream.

Makes 8 to 10 servings.

Marilyn Price
Gonzales, Texas

Tip: *Use an electric knife when possible and/or appropriate.*

I couldn't have done it without Warm Springs. I'd recommend to anyone who's had a stroke to get into a place like Warm Springs as soon as possible. The best time to start is when your inabilities are fresh.

Jim Allen, former stroke patient,
New Braunfels, Texas

Mother's Tamale Pie

2	cups water
1	cup cornmeal
1	tablespoon salt
1	pound ground beef
½	cup chopped onion
⅓	cup chopped green bell pepper
1	tablespoon flour
1	(16-ounce) can tomatoes
½	cup chopped black olives
2	teaspoons chili powder
1	teaspoon salt
¼	teaspoon garlic salt
½	cup shredded Cheddar cheese

Grease the bottom and sides of a shallow baking dish. Combine the water, cornmeal and salt in a saucepan. Cook until thickened, stirring frequently. Shape the cornmeal mixture to cover the bottom and sides of the prepared dish. Brown the ground beef with the onion and green pepper in a skillet, stirring until the ground beef is crumbly; drain. Stir in the flour. Add the tomatoes, olives, chili powder, salt and garlic salt and mix well. Simmer for 5 minutes, stirring frequently. Spoon into the prepared dish. Bake at 350 degrees for 30 minutes. Sprinkle with the cheese. Bake for 5 minutes longer.

Makes 6 to 8 servings.

Jean Beach
El Paso, Texas

Texas Tech Chili

All measurements are approximate. This recipe works best if you "wing it" to taste!

1	(12-ounce) can spicy hot vegetable juice cocktail
1	(10-ounce) can tomato paste
1	(10-ounce) can stewed tomatoes
2	pounds ground beef
1	pound ground pork sausage
2	large white onions, finely chopped
2	green bell peppers, finely chopped
½	cup butter
	White wine to taste
1	envelope Williams chili seasoning
2	tablespoons sugar
1	tablespoon salt
½	teaspoon chili powder
6	(4-ounce) cans chopped green chiles

Combine the vegetable juice cocktail, tomato paste and tomatoes in a stockpot and mix well. Heat to a simmer. Brown the ground beef and sausage in a skillet, stirring until crumbly; drain. Add to the stockpot and mix well. Sauté the onions and green peppers in the butter and white wine in a skillet until tender. Stir into the ground beef mixture. Stir in the chili seasoning, sugar, salt, chili powder and green chiles. Simmer for 4 to 6 hours or until of the desired consistency, stirring occasionally. Ladle into chili bowls.

Makes 8 to 10 servings.

Devin Zakrzewski
San Antonio, Texas

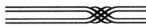

I liked it there, because the people cared about me.

Chris Rivera, former brain-injury patient, Agua Dulce, Texas

Chili Verde

1	(1½-pound) boneless beef chuck roast, cut into 1-inch cubes
1½	pounds lean boneless pork shoulder, cut into 1-inch cubes
3	tablespoons vegetable oil
1	medium green bell pepper, coarsely chopped
1	large clove of garlic, minced, crushed
2	(28-ounce) cans tomatoes
2	(4-ounce) cans chopped green chiles
⅓	cup chopped fresh parsley
2	teaspoons cumin
½	teaspoon sugar
¼	teaspoon ground cloves
1	cup red wine
	Salt to taste
	Lettuce leaves
	Flour tortillas
	Shredded Cheddar cheese

Brown the beef and pork in the oil in a stockpot on all sides. Remove the beef and pork to a platter, reserving the pan drippings. Sauté the green pepper and garlic in the reserved pan drippings until tender. Combine the undrained tomatoes, chiles, parsley, cumin, sugar and cloves in a blender container. Process until blended. Add to the green pepper mixture and mix well. Stir in the beef, pork and wine. Simmer for 2 hours or until of the desired consistency, stirring occasionally. Season with salt. Serve on a bed of lettuce resting on flour tortillas on a platter. Sprinkle with cheese. May substitute a mixture of ¾ cup beef broth and ¼ cup lemon juice for the red wine.

Makes 10 to 12 servings.

Vernie Gomez
Phoenix, Arizona

Orange-Glazed Pork Roast

- 2 tablespoons flour
- 2/3 cup orange juice
- 1 teaspoon instant chicken bouillon granules
- 1/2 teaspoon cinnamon
- 1 (2 1/2- to 3 1/2-pound) pork sirloin roast, bone-in
- 1/2 teaspoon thyme
  Salt and pepper to taste
- 1 small acorn squash, cut into halves, cut into 3/4-inch slices
- 1 large apple, cut into eighths

Add the flour to an oven-cooking bag, shaking to coat the inside. Place the bag in a 9x13-inch baking pan. Add the orange juice, bouillon granules and cinnamon to the bag, shaking to mix. Rub the roast with the thyme, salt and pepper. Place in the prepared bag. Arrange the squash and apple around the roast. Secure the bag with a nylon tie; cut six 1/2-inch slits in the top of the bag. Insert a meat thermometer through one of the slits into the thickest part of the roast. Bake at 325 degrees for 1 1/4 to 1 3/4 hours or until the meat thermometer registers 160 degrees. Let stand in the bag for 5 minutes. Remove the roast, squash and apple to a serving platter.

Makes 4 to 6 servings.

Bobbie Hetrick
Blanco, Texas

Jamaican Spiced Pork Tenderloin with Sweet Potato Purée

½	cup coarsely chopped onion
2	tablespoons white vinegar
1	tablespoon soy sauce
1	tablespoon vegetable oil
½	teaspoon allspice
½	teaspoon salt
¼	teaspoon freshly grated nutmeg
¼	teaspoon cinnamon
⅛	teaspoon cayenne
1	clove of garlic, chopped
12	ounces pork tenderloin, trimmed
	Sweet Potato Purée

Process the onion, vinegar, soy sauce, oil, allspice, salt, nutmeg, cinnamon, cayenne and garlic in a blender until smooth. Pour into a shallow dish. Add the pork, turning to coat. Drain, reserving the spice mixture. Heat a well-seasoned ridged grill pan over medium-high heat just until smoking. Grill the pork until brown on all sides, turning and basting with the reserved spice mixture occasionally. Remove the pork to a shallow greased baking pan. Roast at 450 degrees for 5 to 10 minutes or until cooked through. Remove the pork to a cutting board and tent with foil. Let stand for 5 minutes. Cut the pork diagonally into ½-inch slices. Serve with the Sweet Potato Purée.
 Makes 2 servings.

Sweet Potato Purée

1	pound sweet potatoes
2	tablespoons unsalted butter, softened
2	tablespoons sour cream
1	tablespoon brown sugar
	Salt to taste

Cook or microwave the sweet potatoes until tender; peel. Process the sweet potatoes, butter, sour cream and brown sugar in a blender until smooth. Season with salt.

Shirley Becker
San Antonio, Texas

Tip: *A cutting board with nails may help stabilize food to be cut or peeled.*

Floating Chops with Fruit-Filled Squash

1	or 2 red or green apples, sliced
½	cup fruit nectar
2	tablespoons honey
¼	teaspoon nutmeg
¼	teaspoon cinnamon
	Ground cloves to taste
16	to 20 ounces water
8	to 10 ounces lemon juice
8	to 10 ounces orange juice
3	to 4 cups rice
6	to 8 pork chops, trimmed
3	or 4 acorn squash, cut lengthwise into halves
	Butter

Combine the apples, fruit nectar, honey, nutmeg, cinnamon and cloves in a bowl and mix gently. Combine the water, lemon juice, orange juice and rice in a bowl and mix well. Pour into a 3-quart baking dish. Brown the pork chops in a nonstick skillet on both sides. Arrange the chops over the rice mixture. Let stand for 15 minutes to allow the flavors to marry. Bake at 350 degrees for 40 minutes or until the liquid is absorbed, the rice is tender and the pork chops are cooked through. Place the squash cut side down on a microwave-safe plate. Microwave for 7 minutes or until tender. Turn the squash cut side up. Spoon the apple mixture into the squash. Microwave, covered with plastic wrap, for 16 to 20 minutes or until done to taste. Dot with butter. Serve with the pork chops and rice.

Makes 6 to 8 servings.

Vanessa Ireland
San Antonio, Texas

MAIN DISHES 55

Rosemary-and-Serrano-Roasted Pork Tenderloin

8	red or green serranos
½	cup chopped fresh rosemary
¼	cup soy sauce
¼	cup minced garlic
3	tablespoons cracked pepper
¼	cup peanut oil
½	cup fine bread crumbs
	Salt to taste
1	(3-pound) pork tenderloin

Combine the serranos, rosemary, soy sauce, garlic and pepper in a food processor container. Process until mixed. Add the peanut oil gradually, processing constantly until blended. Add the bread crumbs. Process until mixed. Sprinkle salt over the pork tenderloin. Press the serrano mixture evenly over the pork. Place in a baking pan. Roast at 350 degrees for 50 minutes or until cooked through.

Makes 8 servings.

Susan Hall
San Antonio, Texas

Dear Friends, . . . and I call you friends because, after talking to my mother on the phone just now, I am indebted to you. My mother is eighty-eight and a very dear part of a large and caring family. She is an extraordinary person and has lived a life of devotion and caring to her family. And now, when she is recuperating from her hip surgery, it means so much to me that she is being cared for by a sensitive, loving staff. She tells how patient and kind everyone is–from the doctors, nurses, aides, and therapists. Please give each of them my thanks.

My sister and brother-in-law live in San Antonio while the rest of us are scattered over the states. After their description of Warm Springs, we were so relieved that our mom and grandmother would be able to receive her therapy with you.

Please see that those involved in my mother's care see this letter, and tell the administrator I think you all deserve a raise. God bless you in your service.

Sylvia Fleming, San Antonio, Texas

Grilled Leg of Lamb

- 1 cup olive oil
- 2/3 cup lemon juice
- 2 teaspoons salt
- 1 1/2 teaspoons sage
- 1 1/2 teaspoons thyme
- 1 1/2 teaspoons rosemary
- 3 cloves of garlic
- 6 sprigs of parsley
- 2 bay leaves
- 1 (6- to 7-pound) leg of lamb, butterflied
- Wine Sauce

Combine the olive oil, lemon juice, salt, sage, thyme, rosemary, garlic, parsley and bay leaves in a bowl and mix well. Pour over the lamb in a shallow dish, turning to coat. Marinate, covered, in the refrigerator for 24 hours, turning occasionally. Drain, reserving the marinade. Grill the lamb over hot coals or broil for 15 to 20 minutes on each side or until done to taste, turning and basting with the reserved marinade frequently. Remove to a platter. Slice and serve with the Wine Sauce.

Makes 8 to 12 servings.

Tip: *If meat requires tenderizing or cutting into pieces, have the butcher do it.*

Wine Sauce

- 2 tablespoons chopped shallots
- 1/2 cup beef stock
- 1/4 cup red wine
- 1 1/2 teaspoons rosemary
- 1 1/2 teaspoons sage
- 1 1/2 teaspoons thyme
- 3 tablespoons butter
- 3 tablespoons chopped fresh parsley

Simmer the shallots in the stock and red wine in a saucepan, stirring occasionally. Add the rosemary, sage and thyme and mix well. Simmer for several minutes, stirring occasionally; strain. Stir in the butter and parsley. Simmer just until the butter melts, stirring constantly.

Heidi Schoenfeld
San Antonio, Texas

MAIN DISHES 57

I still have friends in Gonzales that I keep close ties with, and my time there at Warm Springs was so rewarding. I think we really did a tremendous amount of good.

Loraine Millican, first Warm Springs physical therapist, Corpus Christi, Texas

All-In-One

1	(4-ounce) boneless skinless chicken breast
1/2	cup finely chopped carrot
1/2	cup finely chopped celery
1/2	cup finely chopped zucchini
1	tablespoon finely chopped onion
1	tablespoon chopped fresh parsley
1	tablespoon melted margarine
1	tablespoon Dijon mustard
1	tablespoon lemon juice
1/2	teaspoon tarragon
1/2	teaspoon pepper
1/4	cup chopped cucumber
2	tablespoons nonfat yogurt
1	teaspoon finely chopped green onions
1/4	teaspoon dillweed
1/8	teaspoon grated lemon peel

Rinse the chicken and pat dry. Pound between sheets of waxed paper with a meat mallet until flattened. Place the chicken on a 12x18-inch sheet of foil. Layer the carrot, celery, zucchini, onion and parsley over the chicken. Drizzle with a mixture of the margarine, Dijon mustard, lemon juice, tarragon and pepper. Fold the foil to enclose the chicken. Place on a baking sheet. Bake at 450 degrees for 20 minutes or until the chicken is cooked through. Remove the chicken to a dinner plate; discard the foil. Top with a mixture of the cucumber, yogurt, green onions, dillweed and lemon peel. May substitute fish for the chicken and bake for 15 minutes or until the fish flakes easily. May substitute slightly cooked rice for the chicken.

Makes 1 serving.

Suesy Thomas
Gonzales, Texas

Chicken and Dumplings

1	(3½-pound) chicken, cut up
5½	cups water
	Salt and pepper to taste
1¾	cups flour
½	teaspoon baking soda
¼	teaspoon salt
3	tablespoons shortening
⅔	to ¾ cup buttermilk

Rinse the chicken. Combine the chicken, water and salt and pepper to taste in a stockpot. Cook for 30 to 35 minutes or until the chicken is tender. Combine the flour, baking soda and ¼ teaspoon salt in a bowl and mix well. Cut in the shortening until crumbly. Add just enough buttermilk to form a soft dough and mix well; do not overwork the dough. Roll the dough into an 8x8½-inch square on a lightly floured surface. Cut into sixteen 2-inch squares. Bring the chicken and broth to a simmer; do not boil. Slide the dumplings gently into the liquid. Cook for 5 minutes or until the dumplings are puffy and cake-like and cooked through.

Makes 4 servings.

Emma G. Miller
Ganado, Texas

Chicken Creole

1	(3 1/2-pound) chicken, cut up
1/4	cup olive oil
1	(32-ounce) can tomatoes
1	tablespoon butter
1	teaspoon salt
	Black pepper to taste
	Cayenne to taste
1	tablespoon minced fresh parsley
1	sprig of thyme
1	bay leaf
3	cloves of garlic, minced
1	tablespoon butter
1	tablespoon flour
6	shallots, chopped, or 1/2 cup minced onion
5	tablespoons chopped green bell pepper
1/2	cup white wine
	Hot cooked rice
	Sliced avocado
	Sprigs of parsley

Rinse the chicken and pat dry. Sauté the chicken in the olive oil in a skillet until brown on all sides; drain. Combine the tomatoes and 1 tablespoon butter in a saucepan. Simmer for 10 minutes, stirring occasionally. Stir in the salt, black pepper and cayenne. Cook for 10 minutes, stirring occasionally. Add the parsley, thyme, bay leaf and garlic and mix well. Cook for 15 minutes, stirring occasionally. Heat 1 tablespoon butter in a saucepan until melted. Stir in the flour. Cook until brown, stirring constantly. Add the shallots and green pepper. Cook until light brown, stirring constantly. Stir in the white wine. Cook just until the mixture begins to thicken, stirring constantly. Stir into the tomato mixture. Pour over the chicken in the skillet. Simmer, covered, for 45 minutes or until the chicken is cooked through, stirring occasionally. Discard the bay leaf. Spoon over hot cooked rice on a serving platter. Top with avocado slices and sprigs of fresh parsley.

Makes 4 to 5 servings.

Marcia Moore
Austin, Texas

Tip: *Use oven mitts on both hands and place hands under the pan when lifting it instead of using your fingers to lift. A wooden oven shovel or paddle is about 16 inches long and reaches into the stove to help pull a hot pan to the front where you can pick it up more easily.*

Chicken à la Français

- 1 (8-ounce) can sliced mushrooms
- 2 tablespoons cornstarch
- 4 boneless skinless chicken breasts
- 1 teaspoon salt
- ¼ teaspoon pepper
- 2 tablespoons butter
- 1 cup sliced green onions with tops
- 1½ cups chicken broth
- 1 cup green peas
- ½ cup cooking sherry
- 3 tomatoes, peeled, cut into 8 pieces
- 3 cups hot cooked rice

Drain the mushrooms, reserving the liquid. Combine the reserved liquid and cornstarch in a small bowl and mix well. Rinse the chicken and pat dry; cut into thin strips. Season with the salt and pepper. Sauté the chicken in the butter in a skillet until brown on both sides. Add the green onions and mushrooms. Cook for 2 minutes, stirring frequently. Stir in the broth, peas and sherry. Simmer, covered, for 20 minutes. Add the tomatoes and mix well. Stir in the cornstarch mixture. Cook for 5 minutes longer, stirring frequently. Spoon over the hot cooked rice on a serving platter.
    Makes 6 servings.

Vicki Fisher
New Braunfels, Texas

Tip: *Use lightweight, easy-to-clean cookware.*

MAIN DISHES 61

Honey Mustard Chicken

2	(3½-pound) chickens, cut up
½	cup butter
½	cup honey
¼	cup Dijon mustard
1	teaspoon curry powder
½	teaspoon salt

Rinse the chicken and pat dry. Arrange in a shallow baking pan. Heat the butter in a saucepan until melted. Stir in the honey, Dijon mustard, curry powder and salt. Cook just until heated through, stirring frequently. Brush the glaze over the chicken. Bake at 350 degrees for 1½ hours or until the chicken is golden brown and cooked through, basting frequently with the glaze.

Makes 8 to 10 servings.

Isabelle Hall
Lubbock, Texas

Little Red Hen

1½	to 2 pounds chicken pieces
1	(10-ounce) can tomato soup
¼	cup vinegar
2	tablespoons brown sugar
1	teaspoon salt
1	cup chopped onion
1	cup chopped green bell pepper
	Hot cooked rice or noodles

Rinse the chicken and pat dry. Arrange in a shallow baking dish. Combine the soup, vinegar, brown sugar and salt in a bowl and mix well. Stir in the onion and green pepper. Pour over the chicken. Bake at 350 degrees for 1½ hours or until the chicken is cooked through. Serve over hot cooked rice or noodles. May cover loosely with foil to prevent splattering. Remove foil 20 minutes before end of cooking process to allow chicken to brown.

Makes 4 to 6 servings.

Sharon Kuhn
Helotes, Texas

I know it sounds strange, but my life is definitely better now than it was before the accident. I'm much more organized and directed. And I know the positive conquers.

Kevin Logan, former brain-injury patient, New Braunfels, Texas

Aunt Patty's Sopa

1/2	cup chopped onion
2	or 3 cloves of garlic, minced
4	cups chopped cooked chicken or turkey
1	(15-ounce) can tomatoes
2	(4-ounce) cans whole green chiles, drained, chopped
1/2	cup tomato juice
1	(10-ounce) can tomatoes with green chiles
12	corn tortillas, cut into 1-inch slices
1	cup vegetable oil
8	ounces Longhorn cheese, shredded
8	ounces Monterey Jack cheese, shredded
2	cups sour cream

Sauté the onion and garlic in a nonstick skillet. Add the chicken, tomatoes, chiles, tomato juice and tomatoes with green chiles. Simmer for 10 to 15 minutes, stirring frequently. Fry the tortilla strips in the oil in a skillet until soft. Drain and pat dry with a paper towel. Line the bottom of a greased 9x13-inch baking dish with 1/2 of the tortilla strips, overlapping the edges. Layer with 1/2 of the tomato sauce, 1/2 of the Longhorn cheese and 1/2 of the Monterey Jack cheese. Repeat the process with the remaining tortilla strips, tomato sauce, Longhorn cheese and Monterey Jack cheese. Bake at 350 degrees for 40 minutes. Spread with the sour cream. Bake for 5 minutes longer.

Makes 10 to 12 servings.

*Submitted by Nancy Hunt
in memory of Patty Janzen
El Paso, Texas*

Blake's progress should not be seen as a miracle because we expect to continue therapy for an extended time. But there's so much more hope now because Diane Wallace, occupational therapist, and Warm Springs have provided him with an incredibly loving place to grow.

Becky Darilek, mother of pediatric patient, San Antonio, Texas

Chicken Potpie

8	pastry shells
4	cups water
2	cups finely chopped celery
2	cups chopped peeled carrots
½	cup chopped green bell pepper
1	large onion, finely chopped
1	large potato, finely chopped
4	chicken bouillon cubes
1	(10-ounce) can cream of mushroom soup
1	(10-ounce) can cream of chicken soup
2	bay leaves
4	large boneless skinless chicken breasts, cooked, chopped
4	ounces chopped mushrooms
2	to 3 teaspoons chopped fresh parsley
½	cup frozen peas

Bake the pastry shells using package directions. Combine the water, celery, carrots, green pepper, onion, potato and bouillon cubes in a stockpot. Bring to a boil; reduce heat. Simmer for 10 minutes, stirring occasionally. Stir in the soups and bay leaves. Simmer for 20 minutes or until the potato is tender. Add the chicken, mushrooms and parsley and mix well. Simmer for 20 minutes, stirring occasionally. Add the peas just before serving. Discard the bay leaves. Arrange the pastry shells on a serving platter. Spoon the chicken mixture into the shells. Serve immediately. For a thicker consistency add a mixture of 1 teaspoon cornstarch and a small amount of water.

Makes 8 servings.

Diane Stoffer
San Antonio, Texas

Chicken with Rice

1	cup uncooked rice
1	(2- to 2½-pound) chicken, cut up
	Salt and pepper to taste
	Seasoned salt to taste
	Parsley flakes to taste
2	(10-ounce) cans cream of mushroom soup
1½	soup cans water
1	teaspoon lemon juice
1	teaspoon Worcestershire sauce

Line a 10x14-inch baking pan with foil; grease the foil lightly. Spread the rice in the prepared pan. Rinse the chicken and pat dry. Season with salt, pepper, seasoned salt, parsley flakes and any other herbs as desired. Combine the soup, water, lemon juice and Worcestershire sauce in a bowl and mix well. Spoon ½ of the soup mixture over the rice. Arrange the chicken over the top. Spread with the remaining soup mixture. Bake, covered, at 350 degrees for 1 hour or until the chicken is cooked through and the rice is tender. May sauté 3 chopped green onions, 1 chopped rib of celery and 3 or 4 large chopped mushrooms in 1 to 2 tablespoons butter and mix with the rice.

Makes 4 to 5 servings.

Barbara Blair
Lakehills, Texas

Ida Helen Pieper
Cuero, Texas

Dorothy Stoeltje
Seguin, Texas

Thank you for giving me the opportunity to repay Warm Springs (by submitting a recipe), in a very minute way, for all the TLC I received as a patient in 1988. I pray God will continue to bless this endeavor and all the people who make it work.

Christine Sommers, former patient, San Antonio, Texas

Easy Hot Chicken Salad

2	cups chopped cooked chicken or turkey
1	cup chopped celery
1/2	cup chopped green bell pepper
1/4	cup slivered almonds
1	tablespoon grated onion
1/2	(10-ounce) can cream of chicken soup
1/4	cup mayonnaise
1	tablespoon lemon juice
	Crushed potato chips
1/2	cup (or more) shredded cheese

Combine the chicken, celery, green pepper, almonds and onion in a bowl and mix well. Stir in a mixture of the soup, mayonnaise and lemon juice. Spoon into a 1 3/4-quart buttered baking dish. Sprinkle with the potato chips and cheese. Bake at 350 degrees for 30 minutes or until bubbly. May prepare in advance and freeze before baking for future use. Sprinkle with the potato chips and cheese after the dish has been heated through and bake just until the cheese melts.
Makes 4 servings.

Christine Sommers
San Antonio, Texas

Hot Chicken Salad

- 3 whole boneless skinless chicken breasts, cooked, chopped
- 1 (15-ounce) can French-style green beans, drained
- 1 (8-ounce) can water chestnuts, drained, sliced
- 1 (4-ounce) can mushrooms, drained
- 2 cups chopped celery
- 2 tablespoons dried onion flakes
- 2 cups mayonnaise
- 1 (10-ounce) can cream of mushroom soup
- 5 ounces stuffing mix
  Melted butter

Combine the chicken, green beans, water chestnuts, mushrooms, celery and onion flakes in a bowl and mix gently. Stir in a mixture of the mayonnaise and soup. Spoon into a 9x13-inch baking dish. Top with a mixture of the stuffing mix and melted butter. Bake at 350 degrees for 30 minutes. May sprinkle with crushed potato chips instead of the butter and stuffing mixture.

Makes 8 servings.

Betty J. Rogers
San Antonio, Texas

Tip: *Use a kitchen or utility cart to transport items and eliminate extra trips such as when setting the table or unloading groceries.*

Green Enchiladas

Shredded Longhorn cheese
12 corn tortillas
1 pound ground chicken or beef
1 large onion, chopped
2 (10-ounce) cans cream of chicken soup
1 cup sour cream
2 (4-ounce) cans chopped green chiles
Shredded cheese

Spoon shredded Longhorn cheese in the middle of each corn tortilla; roll to enclose the cheese. Arrange the filled tortillas in a 9x12-inch baking dish. Brown the chicken with the onion in a nonstick skillet, stirring until the chicken is crumbly; drain. Stir in the soup, sour cream and chiles. Spoon over the filled tortillas. Sprinkle with shredded cheese. Bake at 350 degrees for 30 minutes.

Makes 6 servings.

Isabelle Hall
Lubbock, Texas

Chicken and Spaghetti

1 (4- to 5-pound) chicken
16 ounces spaghetti
8 ribs celery, chopped
1 green bell pepper, chopped
1 large onion, chopped
2 cloves of garlic, chopped
1 tablespoon vegetable oil
1 (20-ounce) can tomatoes
1 (10-ounce) can cream of mushroom soup
1 cup chopped black olives
16 ounces sharp Cheddar cheese, shredded

Rinse the chicken. Combine the chicken with enough water to cover in a stockpot. Cook until the chicken is tender. Drain, reserving the broth. Chop the chicken, discarding the skin and bones. Cook the spaghetti in the reserved broth in the stockpot until al dente; drain. Sauté the celery, green pepper, onion and garlic in the oil in a skillet until brown. Stir in the tomatoes, soup and olives. Cook over medium heat for 15 to 20 minutes, stirring frequently. Add the chicken and mix well. Spoon the spaghetti into a 3-quart baking dish. Top with the chicken mixture; sprinkle with the cheese. Bake at 350 degrees for 30 minutes. May substitute one 10-ounce can tomatoes with green chiles for the canned tomatoes and Parmesan cheese for the Cheddar cheese.

Makes 6 to 8 servings.

Virginia Grant
San Antonio, Texas

Shirley Loban
San Antonio, Texas

Chicken and Spaghetti in Wine Sauce

- 3 pounds chicken pieces
- 2 tablespoons vegetable oil
- ¼ cup margarine
- 1 cup chopped onion
- 1 cup chopped celery
- 1 cup chopped carrot
- 1 (16-ounce) can Italian tomatoes
- 1 (6-ounce) can tomato paste
- ¾ cup dry wine
- 2 teaspoons salt
- ½ teaspoon pepper
- 8 ounces spaghetti, cooked, drained

Rinse the chicken and pat dry. Brown the chicken in a mixture of the oil and margarine in a Dutch oven. Remove the chicken with a slotted spoon to a platter, reserving the pan drippings. Sauté the onion, celery and carrot in the reserved pan drippings for 5 minutes. Stir in the undrained tomatoes, tomato paste, wine, salt and pepper. Bring to a boil, stirring constantly; reduce heat. Add the chicken and mix well. Simmer, covered, for 1½ hours or until the chicken is cooked through, stirring occasionally. Arrange the spaghetti on a serving platter. Top with the chicken; drizzle with the sauce.
  Makes 6 servings.

Vickie Odom
Benton, Louisiana

I'd never seen a hospital like that before. They had decorated the children's room and even had Dalmatian sheets on the beds. They even had sandwiches made for us because we arrived late.

Cammie Avants, mother of two former pediatric brain-injury/ orthopedic-injury patients, San Antonio, Texas

Yorkshire Chicken

1	(3½-pound) chicken, cut up
⅓	cup flour
2	teaspoons salt
1½	teaspoons sage
¼	teaspoon pepper
	Vegetable oil
2	cups sifted flour
2	teaspoons baking powder
2	teaspoons salt
6	eggs
3	cups milk
½	cup melted margarine
¼	cup chopped fresh parsley

Rinse the chicken and pat dry. Combine ⅓ cup flour, 2 teaspoons salt, sage and pepper in a bowl and mix well. Coat the chicken with the flour mixture. Sauté the chicken in oil in a skillet until brown on all sides; drain. Arrange the chicken in a 2-quart baking dish. Combine 2 cups flour, baking powder and 2 teaspoons salt in a bowl. Stir in a mixture of the eggs, milk, margarine and parsley. Pour over the chicken. Bake at 350 degrees for 1 hour or until light brown and the chicken is cooked through; do not overbake. May substitute dried parsley flakes for chopped fresh parsley. The batter recipe may be cut in half for smaller portions.

Makes 4 to 5 servings.

In memory of Jean Anderson El Paso, Texas

Zesty Oregano Chicken

3	pounds chicken legs
1	tablespoon oregano
1	tablespoon thyme
2	teaspoons grated lemon peel
1	teaspoon salt
½	teaspoon pepper
2	tablespoons olive oil
1	large onion, chopped
3	cloves of garlic, minced
¾	cup white wine
1	cup pitted prunes
¼	cup sliced green olives
¼	cup sliced black olives
¼	cup white wine
1	(14-ounce) can artichokes, drained, rinsed, cut into quarters

Rinse the chicken and pat dry. Sprinkle with a mixture of the oregano, thyme, lemon peel, salt and pepper. Heat the olive oil over high heat in a skillet until hot. Add the chicken. Cook for 5 minutes per side or until brown. Remove the chicken to a platter with a slotted spoon, reserving the pan drippings. Sauté the onion and garlic in the reserved pan drippings for 8 minutes or until tender. Stir in ¾ cup white wine, prunes, olives and chicken. Simmer, covered, for 30 minutes or until the chicken is cooked through, stirring occasionally. Remove the chicken with a slotted spoon to a heated serving platter. Cover to keep warm. Add ¼ cup white wine to the skillet and mix well. Stir in the artichokes. Cook over high heat for 2 to 3 minutes or just until thickened, stirring constantly. Spoon over the chicken. May substitute chicken breasts for the chicken legs, increasing the cooking time.

Makes 6 servings.

Vicki Davis
San Antonio, Texas

Warm Springs is like its own family–its own little world. The people who worked there and continue to work there are special, caring people.

Mary Margaret Lacy, daughter of founding charter board member Frank Boehm, Victoria, Texas

Marinated Turkey

1	(5- to 6-pound) turkey breast
2½	cups white wine cooler
1½	cups pineapple juice
¾	cup soy sauce
¾	cup vegetable oil
1½	teaspoons garlic salt
¾	cup barbecue sauce

Rinse the turkey and pat dry. Cut into ¼- to ½-inch slices. Arrange in a shallow dish. Chill while preparing marinade. Combine the white wine cooler, pineapple juice, soy sauce, oil and garlic salt in a nonreactive bowl and mix well. Reserve ¾ cup of the marinade. Pour the remaining marinade over the turkey, turning to coat. Marinate, covered, in the refrigerator for 24 to 48 hours, turning occasionally. Combine the reserved marinade and barbecue sauce in a bowl and mix well. Drain the turkey, discarding the marinade. Place the turkey on the grill rack over medium-hot coals; brush with the barbecue sauce mixture. Grill with lid closed until the turkey is cooked through, turning and basting with the barbecue sauce mixture frequently.

Makes 12 servings.

Katherine Carlson
Parkers Prairie, Minnesota

Crawfish Etouffée

- 1 large onion, chopped
- ½ green bell pepper, chopped
- 3 or 4 green onions with tops, chopped
- 3 cloves of garlic, minced
- ½ cup butter
- 1 (10-ounce) can cream of mushroom soup
- 16 ounces crawfish, thawed
- Flour (optional)
- Lemon pepper to taste
- Tabasco sauce to taste (optional)
- Hot cooked rice

Sauté the onion, green pepper, green onions and garlic in the butter in a large skillet until tender. Stir in the soup and just enough water to prevent the mixture from sticking. Cook over medium-low heat for 15 to 20 minutes or until of the desired consistency, stirring frequently. Stir in the crawfish and juices. Cook for 10 minutes, stirring occasionally. May add flour for the desired consistency. Season with lemon pepper and Tabasco sauce. Spoon over hot cooked rice.

Makes 4 servings.

Barbara Blair
Lakehills, Texas

Tip: Work with the fingers extended whenever possible.

If I could walk, I wouldn't be me. I wouldn't have done the things that I have. I probably wouldn't have gone to the Paralympics. I've traveled internationally because I'm in a wheelchair. I've met some really cool people because I'm in a wheelchair. It's who I am, and I wouldn't change that.

Ross Davis, Warm Springs Wheelchair Sports coordinator and 1996 International Paralympic gold and bronze medalist in 100m and 400m sprints, San Antonio, Texas

Pescado Picante

2	drum, trout or redfish fillets
	Juice of ½ lemon
¼	cup margarine
2	heads garlic, separated into cloves, crushed
1	jalapeño, seeded, finely chopped
	Salt and ground pepper to taste
	Cilantro leaves to taste
	Dried chopped onions to taste

Arrange the fish fillets on a sheet of heavy-duty foil. Combine the lemon juice, margarine, garlic, jalapeño, salt and pepper in a saucepan. Cook until heated through, stirring frequently. Drizzle over the fillets. Sprinkle with liberal amounts of cilantro and dried onions. Place the fillets on the foil on the grill rack; close the lid. Grill over high heat until the fish flakes easily. Serve with refried beans, flour tortillas and pico de gallo or picante sauce.

Makes 2 servings.

Dolores Gonzalez
Kerrville, Texas

Tuna Noodle Crisp

4	ounces noodles
	Salt to taste
1/3	cup chopped onion
2	tablespoons chopped green bell pepper
1/4	cup vegetable shortening
1	(10-ounce) can cheese soup
1/2	cup milk
1	tablespoon chopped pimento
1	teaspoon salt
1/8	teaspoon pepper
1	(7-ounce) can tuna
1/2	cup bread crumbs

Cook the noodles in boiling salted water in a saucepan using package directions; drain. Sauté the onion and green pepper in the shortening in a skillet until tender; drain. Stir in the soup, milk, pimento, 1 teaspoon salt and pepper. Bring to a boil. Stir in the tuna and noodles. Spoon into a 1 1/2- or 2-quart baking dish. Sprinkle with the bread crumbs. Bake at 350 degrees for 25 to 30 minutes or until bubbly. May microwave on High for 4 minutes.

Makes 4 to 6 servings.

Rita R. Charles
San Antonio, Texas

Tip: *Single-lever faucets reduce excess hand and wrist motion.*

Shrimp Conchiglia

- ½ cup chili sauce
- ½ cup mayonnaise
- 1 tablespoon lemon juice
- ¼ teaspoon garlic powder
- ¼ cup freshly grated Parmesan cheese
- 1 pound cooked shrimp, peeled, deveined
- 6 baked pastry shells
- Parmesan cheese to taste

Combine the chili sauce, mayonnaise, lemon juice, garlic powder and ¼ cup Parmesan cheese in a bowl and mix well. Stir in the shrimp. Spoon into the pastry shells. Top each shell with a small amount of Parmesan cheese. Arrange on a baking sheet. Broil until bubbly. Serve with French bread. May prepare in advance, store in the refrigerator and broil just before serving.

Makes 6 servings.

Jo Ann Wigodsky
San Antonio, Texas

Spicy Camp Shrimp

- 1 medium onion, chopped
- 3 serranos, chopped
- 3 cloves of garlic, minced
- ¼ cup butter
- 1 (8-ounce) can tomato sauce
- 1 cup water
- 1 bay leaf
- ½ teaspoon sugar
- ½ teaspoon salt
- ½ teaspoon red pepper
- Juice of 1 lemon
- 2 pounds peeled shrimp
- Hot cooked brown or wild rice

Sauté the onion, serranos and garlic in the butter in a skillet until the onion is tender. Stir in the tomato sauce, water, bay leaf, sugar, salt, red pepper and lemon juice. Simmer for 10 minutes, stirring occasionally. Add the shrimp and mix well. Cook over low heat for 30 minutes or until the shrimp are pink and the mixture is of the desired consistency, stirring occasionally. Discard the bay leaf. Serve over hot cooked brown or wild rice.

Makes 6 to 8 servings.

A Friend of Warm Springs

Shrimp and Lobster with Wild Rice

1½	cups water
½	cup wild rice
½	teaspoon salt
8	ounces fresh mushrooms, sliced
1	cup chopped celery
1	green bell pepper, chopped
1	medium onion, finely chopped
¼	cup butter
10	ounces lobster tails, cooked, chopped
1½	pounds cooked shrimp, peeled
2	(10-ounce) cans cream of mushroom soup
¼	cup cream
¼	cup sherry
2	ounces chopped pimento
½	cup slivered almonds, toasted

Combine the water, wild rice and salt in a saucepan. Cook using package directions. Cook the mushrooms, celery, green pepper and onion in the butter in a skillet for 10 minutes, stirring frequently. Stir in the lobster and shrimp. Add the rice, soup, cream, sherry and pimento and mix well. Spoon into a greased baking dish. Top with the almonds. Bake at 350 degrees for 45 minutes.

Makes 6 servings.

Linda Lee Davis
San Antonio, Texas

Tip: For pushing items, rest your hand on the table or surface and slide the object along.

Rio Grande Shrimp

36	large or medium shrimp, peeled, deveined, split into halves
	Flour
1	egg, beaten
	Cracker crumbs
3/4	cup melted butter or margarine
1	tablespoon Worcestershire sauce
1	clove of garlic, minced

Coat the shrimp with flour; dip in the egg. Roll in cracker crumbs. Arrange on a baking sheet. Mix the butter, Worcestershire sauce and garlic in a bowl. Pour over the shrimp. Bake at 400 degrees for 5 minutes on each side or until the shrimp turn pink. May prepare ahead, cover and store in the refrigerator until just before serving. Pour the butter mixture over the shrimp just before baking.

Makes 6 to 8 servings.

Marsha Orr
New Braunfels, Texas

Shrimp in Sour Cream

2 1/2	pounds shrimp, peeled, deveined
2	shallots, minced
1/2	cup butter
8	ounces mushrooms, sliced
2	tablespoons flour
1	teaspoon salt
	Pepper to taste
2	cups sour cream
1/4	cup vermouth
1	tablespoon brandy
	Hot cooked rice or toast points

Sauté the shrimp and shallots in the butter in a skillet for 5 minutes or until the shrimp are pink. Stir in the mushrooms. Sauté for 5 minutes longer. Stir in the flour, salt and pepper. Add the sour cream gradually, stirring constantly. Cook until thickened, stirring constantly. Remove from heat. Stir in the vermouth and brandy. Serve over hot cooked rice or toast points.

Makes 4 to 6 servings.

Linda Zealy
Victoria, Texas

Tip: *Use the stronger side of your hand (little-finger side) when possible.*

Grilled Shrimp and Vegetables

- 1/4 cup melted butter
- Lemon juice to taste
- 2 pounds large shrimp, peeled, deveined
- 2 tomatoes, finely chopped
- 1 large white onion, finely chopped
- 1 green bell pepper, finely chopped
- 1 red pepper, finely chopped
- 1/4 cup melted butter
- Nature's Seasons seasoning blend
- Pepper to taste
- Hot cooked rice

Pour a mixture of 1/4 cup melted butter and lemon juice to taste over the shrimp in a shallow dish, turning to coat. Marinate, covered, in the refrigerator for 1 to 2 hours, turning occasionally. Combine the tomatoes, onion, green pepper and red pepper in a bowl and mix gently. Pour a mixture of 1/4 cup melted butter and lemon juice to taste over the vegetables, tossing to coat. Sprinkle with the seasonings. Spoon onto a sheet of heavy-duty foil; fold to enclose the vegetables. Grill the vegetable packet over hot coals for 35 to 45 minutes or until the vegetables are done to taste. Drain the shrimp, discarding the marinade. Grill the shrimp over hot coals until the shrimp are pink, turning occasionally. Arrange the shrimp and vegetables over hot cooked rice on a serving platter.

Makes 6 servings.

Devin Zakrzewski
San Antonio, Texas

Grilled Swordfish

½	cup packed fresh parsley leaves
2	tablespoons drained capers
1½	tablespoons fresh lemon juice
1	tablespoon Dijon mustard
1	large clove of garlic
¼	cup olive oil
	Salt and pepper to taste
6	(8-ounce) swordfish steaks, ½ inch thick
½	cup olive oil

Process the parsley, capers, lemon juice, Dijon mustard, garlic, ¼ cup olive oil, salt and pepper in a food processor until finely minced but not smooth. May be prepared 3 hours in advance and stored, covered, at room temperature. Brush both sides of the swordfish with ½ cup olive oil. Place the steaks on an oiled grill rack. Grill over hot coals for 2 minutes on each side or until the fish flakes easily. Arrange the steaks on a serving platter. Serve with the salsa verde.

Makes 6 servings.

Susan Hall
San Antonio, Texas

Tip: *For less hand strain, hold all tool and utensil handles with a grasp that maintains your knuckles parallel to the handle.*

Success Is Independence — Warm Springs Long-Term Supported Living

The Warm Springs Rehabilitation System recently celebrated the grand opening of the M. G. and Lillie A. Johnson and Area Cattlemen Residence located on the campus of Gonzales Warm Springs Rehabilitation Hospital. The home was finished in the fall of 1995, marking the end of an extensive fund-raising and construction project. The home was designed as the first in a series of proposed homes to create permanent on-campus accommodations for individuals with brain injury who are unable to return to independent living. The residence is so-named in honor of its major donors: the M. G. and Lillie A. Johnson Foundation of Victoria and the Gonzales area cattlemen.

Eight long-term residents moved into the building immediately from accommodations in the hospital. According to John Davis, Gonzales Warm Springs administrator, the home represents a special opportunity for the clients.

"This new residence is a beautiful, peaceful place," he says. "When you realize that these people call this place 'home,' you understand how important it is that it be the very best. Many of these people will spend the rest of their lives as members of the Warm Springs family and this community, and I think the clients' families will be pleased to see what we've all worked together to accomplish."

In addition to supervised and/or assisted living conditions, the program also features supported employment opportunities, leisure and on-site recreational activities, supervised community outings, health and wellness programming, family counseling and training, and access to physician and medical support services. It is available on a referral basis to clients who meet specific criteria. For more information, call (210) 672-6592.

Side Dishes & Breads

At Warm Springs, long-term supported living means much more than assistance with daily activities. It's a safe, serene setting full of opportunity for vocational endeavor and social interaction, with access to the best medical professionals.

Carrots Amandine

1   pound carrots, peeled, thinly sliced
1/4   cup golden raisins
1/4   cup I Can't Believe It's Not Butter!
3   tablespoons honey
1   tablespoon lemon juice
1/4   teaspoon ground ginger
1/4   cup sliced unpeeled almonds

Combine the carrots with enough boiling water to cover by 1/2 inch in a saucepan. Cook for 8 minutes; drain. Stir in the raisins, I Can't Believe It's Not Butter!, honey, lemon juice and ginger. Spoon into a 1-quart baking dish. Bake at 375 degrees for 35 minutes, stirring occasionally. Spoon into a serving bowl; sprinkle with the almonds.

    Makes 4 servings.

A Friend of Warm Springs

Copper Coins

6   cups sliced carrots
1   green bell pepper, chopped
1/4   cup vegetable oil
1   teaspoon dry mustard
     Salt and pepper to taste

Combine the carrots with enough water to cover in a saucepan. Bring to a boil. Boil for 5 minutes or until tender-crisp; drain. Combine the carrots, green pepper, oil, dry mustard, salt and pepper in a bowl and mix gently. Chill, covered, for 2 hours or longer.

    Makes 8 to 10 servings.

Hazel Duncan
San Antonio, Texas

Cheesy Cauliflower

1	medium head cauliflower, trimmed
1/4	cup mayonnaise
2	teaspoons Dijon mustard
3/4	cup shredded cheese

Steam the cauliflower in a steamer for 10 to 15 minutes or until tender. Place in a 2-quart baking dish. Spread the cauliflower with a mixture of the mayonnaise and Dijon mustard; sprinkle with the cheese. Bake at 375 degrees for 10 minutes or until the cheese melts.

Makes 4 servings.

Barbara Otto
Shiner, Texas

Tip: Use a mounted jar opener, and use both hands around the jar when opening it.

Hudson's on the Bend Corn Pudding

1	green bell pepper, chopped
1	red bell pepper, chopped
1	Anaheim pepper or serrano, chopped
1 1/2	cups flour
1/2	cup sugar
5	tablespoons baking powder
3/4	tablespoon salt
1 1/2	teaspoons cayenne
10	eggs
2	(9-ounce) cans cream-style corn
1	cup whipping cream
3/4	cup melted butter
2	pounds fresh or frozen whole kernel corn

Combine the bell peppers and Anaheim pepper in a bowl and mix well. Combine the flour, sugar, baking powder, salt and cayenne in a bowl and mix well. Whisk the eggs in a bowl lightly. Add the cream-style corn, whipping cream and butter, whisking until mixed. Add the egg mixture to the flour mixture gradually, stirring constantly until mixed. Stir in the bell pepper mixture and whole kernel corn. Spoon into a 9x13-inch greased and floured baking dish. Bake at 375 degrees for 40 to 45 minutes or until set and golden brown.

Makes 16 to 20 servings.

Dorothy Ploeger
Gonzales, Texas

Corn and Noodle Casserole

- 1 onion, chopped
- 1 (6-ounce) can (or more) mushrooms, drained
- ½ to 1 green or red bell pepper, chopped (optional)
- ¼ to ½ cup butter or margarine
- 2 or 3 (16-ounce) cans whole kernel corn, drained
- 1 package small noodles or shells, cooked, drained
- Salt and pepper to taste
- Paprika to taste

Sauté the onion, mushrooms and green pepper in the butter in a skillet. Stir in the corn and noodles. Season with salt and pepper. Spoon into a buttered baking dish. Sprinkle with paprika. Bake at 350 degrees for 20 to 30 minutes or until bubbly. May substitute Mexicorn for the whole kernel corn and fresh mushrooms for the canned mushrooms.

Makes 8 to 10 servings.

Abbi Michelson
Lockhart, Texas

Tip: *Use a wrist loop (rope) to decrease stress on your fingers when opening cabinets, drawers, or doors.*

Corn Casserole

- 2 (15-ounce) cans cream-style corn
- 1 (9-ounce) package corn muffin mix
- ¾ cup milk
- ½ cup melted margarine
- ¾ cup shredded mild Cheddar cheese
- 2 eggs, beaten

Combine the corn, muffin mix, milk, margarine, cheese and eggs in a bowl and mix well. Spoon into a 9x12-inch baking dish. Bake at 350 degrees for 45 minutes.

Makes 10 servings.

Pat Eska
Gonzales, Texas

Connie Kuykendall
Luling, Texas

Green Bean Casserole

- 1 cup milk
- 2 eggs, lightly beaten
- 1 cup flour
- 2 teaspoons salt
- 2 teaspoons pepper
- 1 large onion, sliced, separated into rings
- 2 cups vegetable oil
- 4 cups whipping cream
- 1 cup chicken stock
- 1 tablespoon nutmeg
- 1 pound fresh green beans, trimmed, blanched
- 1 pound Swiss or provolone cheese, shredded

Combine the milk and eggs in a bowl and mix well. Combine the flour, salt and pepper in a bowl and mix well. Coat the onion rings with the flour mixture; dip in the egg mixture. Toss in the flour mixture; shake off the excess flour. Fry the onion rings in the oil in a deep skillet until golden brown; drain. Combine the whipping cream, stock and nutmeg in a saucepan. Cook over medium heat until reduced by ¼, stirring frequently. Remove from heat. Stir in the green beans. Spoon into a baking pan sprayed with nonstick cooking spray. Top with the onion rings; sprinkle with the cheese. Bake, covered, at 350 degrees for 20 minutes.

Makes 6 to 8 servings.

Mark Collins
San Antonio, Texas

Roasted Green Beans

1/2	bag pearl onions
1	pound green beans, trimmed
3	to 4 tablespoons olive oil
6	to 8 medium cloves of garlic, sliced
1/2	teaspoon salt
1	to 2 tablespoons balsamic vinegar
	Pepper to taste

Cook the onions for 3 minutes using package directions; drain. Rinse the green beans. Drain and pat dry. Brush a baking pan with 1/2 of the olive oil. Add the green beans, tossing to coat. Stir in the onions and garlic. Add the salt and mix well. Drizzle with the remaining olive oil. Bake at 400 degrees for 20 to 30 minutes, stirring once. Drizzle with the balsamic vinegar; sprinkle with pepper.

Makes 4 servings.

Mike Mahaffey
Corpus Christi, Texas

Barbecue Potatoes

12	slices bacon
5	pounds potatoes, sliced
1	cup chopped onion
1/2	cup margarine
	Salt and pepper to taste

Lay 2 sheets heavy-duty foil on a hard surface. Arrange 6 slices of the bacon vertically in the middle of the foil. Layer the potatoes and onion alternately over the bacon until all the ingredients are used, dotting with margarine and sprinkling with salt and pepper between each layer. Arrange the remaining 6 slices of bacon on top and seal the foil. Cook over hot coals until the foil is puffed and the potatoes are tender. Slit open the foil to serve.

Makes 12 to 15 servings.

Kimberly Simmons
McCoy, Texas

Olive Oil Mashed Potatoes

2 baking potatoes
2 tablespoons olive oil
  Kosher salt to taste
  Pepper to taste

Microwave the potatoes until tender. Cool slightly. Peel the potatoes. Press the potato pulp through a ricer or mash in a bowl. Add the olive oil, kosher salt and pepper, beating until smooth. Serve immediately.
   Makes 4 servings.

Cathy L. Jones
Dallas, Texas

Tip: *Use electric appliances such as an electric can opener, blender, mixer, or food processor whenever possible and/or appropriate.*

Easy New Potatoes

15 to 18 small new potatoes
½ cup olive oil
1 envelope Italian salad dressing mix

Coat the potatoes with the olive oil. Arrange in a single layer in a baking pan. Sprinkle with the dressing mix. Bake at 400 degrees for 1 hour or until tender. May peel and quarter the potatoes.
   Makes 5 to 6 servings.

Ann Driver
Scotsdale, Arizona

Delicious Potatoes

6 medium unpeeled potatoes
½ cup chopped green onions
1½ cups shredded Cheddar cheese
1 (10-ounce) can cream of chicken soup
¼ cup butter
2 cups sour cream

Combine the potatoes with enough water to cover in a saucepan. Bring to a boil; reduce heat. Cook over medium heat until tender; drain. Peel and coarsely grate or finely chop the potatoes. Combine the potatoes, green onions and cheese in a bowl and mix gently. Combine the soup and butter in a saucepan and mix well. Cook until blended, stirring frequently. Stir in the sour cream. Add to the potato mixture and mix gently. Spoon into a baking dish. Bake at 350 degrees for 45 minutes.
   Makes 6 to 8 servings.

Debra Clark
Toronto, Canada

Spinach Casserole

- 1 (32-ounce) package frozen cut leaf spinach
- 6 ounces cream cheese, cubed
- ½ cup butter or margarine
- Grated peel and juice of 1 lemon
- ½ teaspoon nutmeg
- Salt to taste
- Cayenne to taste
- 1 cup stuffing mix

Cook the spinach using package directions; drain. Squeeze the moisture from the spinach. Combine the cream cheese and butter in a microwave-safe dish. Microwave until blended, stirring frequently. Stir in the spinach. Add the lemon peel, lemon juice, nutmeg, salt and cayenne and mix well. Spoon into a baking pan. Sprinkle the stuffing mix over the top. Bake at 325 degrees for 20 to 25 minutes or until heated through; do not overbake. Serve immediately.

Makes 6 to 8 servings.

Susan Mayfield
El Paso, Texas

Baked Squash Daniel

8	ounces bacon, finely chopped
1	medium green bell pepper, minced
½	medium onion, minced
3	pounds yellow squash, sliced, cooked, drained
4	ounces Cheddar cheese, shredded
½	cup cracker meal
2	eggs, lightly beaten
	Salt and pepper to taste
	Crushed cornflakes

Sauté the bacon, green pepper and onion in a skillet, stirring until the bacon is crisp and the vegetables are tender. Remove from heat. Add the squash, cheese, cracker meal, eggs, salt and pepper, stirring until mixed. Spoon into a greased baking pan. Sprinkle with cornflakes. Bake at 350 degrees for 35 to 40 minutes or until bubbly.

Makes 8 servings.

Emily Ess
Seguin, Texas

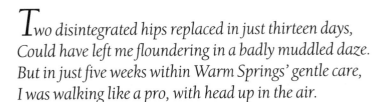

Two disintegrated hips replaced in just thirteen days,
Could have left me floundering in a badly muddled daze.
But in just five weeks within Warm Springs' gentle care,
I was walking like a pro, with head up in the air.

I've walked in the Senior Olympics,
    the Fun Walk don't you know,
And even have a medal, a bronze one, that I can show.

So to the caring, knowing staff who put me on my feet,
I'll praise their name and spread their fame
    to all the folks I meet.

Janice Gates, former hip-replacement patient, San Antonio, Texas

Vegetable Pie

- 1 1/2 cups flour
- 1/2 cup grated Parmesan cheese
- 1 1/2 teaspoons sugar
- 1 teaspoon salt
- 1/2 cup vegetable oil
- 2 tablespoons milk
- Florets of 1 large bunch broccoli
- 1 1/2 cups shredded Monterey Jack cheese
- 1/2 cup grated Parmesan cheese
- 1 bunch green onions, chopped
- 2 tablespoons flour
- 1 tablespoon chopped fresh basil
- 1/2 teaspoon pepper
- 1/2 teaspoon thyme
- 3 or 4 tomatoes, thinly sliced
- 3 tablespoons melted butter or margarine

Combine 1 1/2 cups flour, 1/2 cup Parmesan cheese, sugar and salt in a bowl and mix well. Add the oil and milk, stirring until the mixture forms a ball. Press evenly into a 9-inch pie plate. Cook the broccoli in boiling water in a saucepan until tender-crisp; drain. Combine the Monterey Jack cheese, 1/2 cup Parmesan cheese, green onions, 2 tablespoons flour, basil, pepper and thyme in a bowl and mix well. Spoon 1/2 of the cheese mixture into the prepared pie plate. Layer the broccoli and tomato slices over the prepared layers. Top with the remaining cheese mixture; drizzle with the butter. Bake at 325 degrees for 30 minutes or until the cheese melts and the pie is heated through.

Makes 6 to 8 servings.

Nancy Hunt
San Antonio, Texas

At Warm Springs, they greeted us with open arms. They told us about what we should expect, and we asked a lot of questions. I told her that together we could do this if we took it one day at a time.

Peter Adrian, husband of a former stroke patient, Kingsville, Texas

Sour Cream Onion Pie

2	pounds Spanish onions, thinly sliced
½	cup butter or margarine
1	cup sour cream
3	eggs, beaten
¼	teaspoon salt
½	teaspoon white pepper
⅛	teaspoon Tabasco sauce
1	unbaked (9-inch) pie shell
¾	cup grated Parmesan cheese

Sauté the onions in the butter in a skillet. Remove from heat. Combine the sour cream and eggs in a bowl and mix well. Stir into the onion mixture. Add the salt, white pepper and Tabasco sauce and mix well. Spoon into the pie shell. Sprinkle with Parmesan cheese. Bake at 450 degrees for 20 minutes. Reduce the oven temperature to 325 degrees. Bake for 20 minutes longer. Serve with your favorite steak or favorite cut of beef.

Makes 6 to 8 servings.

Dottie Oliver
Dataw Island, South Carolina

Hot Fruit Compote

- Lemon juice
- 3 or 4 bananas, sliced
- 1 (28-ounce) can peach halves, drained
- 1 (28-ounce) can peach slices, drained
- 1 (15-ounce) can pineapple chunks, drained
- 1 (17-ounce) can apricot halves, drained
- 1 (17-ounce) can Kadota figs, drained
- 1 (15-ounce) can dark red sweet cherries, drained, pitted
- 4 to 6 dozen almond or coconut macaroons, crushed
- 2 packages slivered almonds, toasted
- Brown sugar
- Butter
- 1/3 cup banana liqueur or Cointreau

Drizzle the lemon juice over the bananas in a bowl. Layer the peach halves, peach slices, pineapple chunks, apricot halves, figs, cherries and bananas in a buttered 8x8-inch baking dish. Top with the macaroons and almonds. Sprinkle with the brown sugar; dot with butter. Drizzle the liqueur over the top. Bake at 300 degrees for 20 to 30 minutes or until bubbly.

Makes 10 to 12 servings.

Catherine Spruce
Abilene, Texas

Tip: To avoid strained hands, place a sponge or wet towel under a jar, or set the bottom of the jar inside a drawer and lean against it with your hip. Place the palm of your hand on the jar lid and using the weight of your body, turn your arm at the shoulder to open the jar.

Baked Fruit

2   large cans peach halves
    (16 to 20 peach halves)
1   large can crushed, chunk or
    sliced pineapple
2   tablespoons cornstarch
½   cup packed brown sugar
    Grated peel and juice of
    1 lemon
1   teaspoon curry powder

Drain the peaches and pineapple, reserving the juice. Arrange the peaches in a single layer in an 11x14-inch baking dish. Layer the pineapple over the peaches. May arrange a pineapple slice under each peach half. Dissolve the cornstarch in ¼ cup of the reserved pineapple juice and mix well.

Heat the remaining reserved pineapple juice and reserved peach juice in a saucepan. Stir in the brown sugar, lemon peel, lemon juice and curry powder. Bring to a boil. Stir in the cornstarch mixture. Cook over medium heat until thickened, stirring constantly. Pour the desired amount of the sauce over the fruit. Bake at 350 degrees for 20 minutes or until bubbly.

The leftover sauce may be stored in the refrigerator and served with ham or pork roast. Add a small amount of hot mustard to the sauce for a sweet-and-sour sauce for egg rolls.

Variation: Add 5 or 6 finely chopped stewed dried apricots and 2 teaspoons finely chopped crystallized ginger to the fruit before baking.

Makes 8 to 10 servings.

Carolyn Driver
El Paso, Texas

Chili Cheese Casserole

3   (4-ounce) cans whole green
    chiles, drained
2   cups milk
2   eggs, beaten
⅓   cup flour
8   ounces shredded
    Cheddar cheese
8   ounces shredded
    Monterey Jack cheese

Arrange the chiles in a greased 9-inch pie plate, overlapping as needed to form a shell. Combine the milk and eggs in a bowl and mix well. Whisk in the flour until blended. Pour into the prepared pie plate. Sprinkle with a mixture of the Cheddar cheese and Monterey Jack Cheese. Bake at 350 degrees for 30 minutes or until set and golden brown.

Makes 6 to 8 servings.

Carolyn Driver
El Paso, Texas

Tuscan Fettuccini with Artichokes Stefano

4	to 6 ounces fettuccini
½	cup margarine
5	mushrooms, sliced
1	(14-ounce) can artichokes, drained, cut into halves
10	to 12 medium shrimp, boiled, peeled, deveined
⅓	cup chopped fresh cilantro
2	tablespoons chopped fresh oregano
2	tablespoons minced garlic
2	tablespoons white wine (optional)
½	teaspoon pepper
	Grated Parmesan cheese to taste

Cook the fettuccini using package directions; drain. Heat the margarine in a skillet over medium heat until melted. Add the mushrooms. Sauté for 5 minutes. Stir in the artichokes, shrimp, cilantro, oregano, garlic, white wine and pepper. Cook just until heated through, stirring frequently. Spoon over the hot cooked fettuccini on a serving platter. Sprinkle with grated Parmesan cheese.

Makes 2 servings.

Steve Hahn
San Antonio, Texas

SIDE DISHES 95

Cheese and Tomato Toss

1   (12-ounce) package fettuccini
3   tablespoons margarine
3   tablespoons French vinaigrette salad dressing
3   tomatoes, peeled, chopped
3/4 cup finely shredded mozzarella cheese
1/3 cup grated Parmesan cheese
1/4 cup finely chopped green onions
1 1/2 teaspoons basil
1/2 teaspoon salt
1/4 teaspoon pepper
1   or 2 chopped cooked seasoned chicken breasts (optional)

Prepare the pasta using package directions; drain. Combine the pasta, margarine and salad dressing in a bowl, tossing to coat. Add the tomatoes, mozzarella cheese, Parmesan cheese, green onions, basil, salt and pepper, tossing to mix. Top with the chicken.
   Makes 6 servings.

Vicki Fisher
New Braunfels, Texas

Sun-Dried Tomato Pesto

1   cup chopped fresh basil
6   ounces grated Romano cheese
3/4 cup pine nuts, toasted
3/4 cup olive oil
1/2 cup oil-pack sun-dried tomatoes, drained
1   small red bell pepper, chopped
6   cloves of garlic, roasted
1   teaspoon freshly ground pepper
    Salt to taste

Combine the basil, cheese, pine nuts, olive oil, tomatoes, red pepper, garlic, pepper and salt in a food processor container. Process until chopped but not puréed. Chill, covered, until serving time.
   Makes variable servings.

Cecile McAllister
San Antonio, Texas

*I*n all, I was very pleased with the results of my therapy at Warm Springs, but the therapists were so nice that now I find myself missing them.

Debbie Adrian, former stroke patient, Kingsville, Texas

Spanish Rice

- 2 cups rice
- ¼ cup butter
- ½ cup chopped onion
- 2 tablespoons chopped green bell pepper
- 1 clove of garlic, minced
- 1 (8-ounce) can tomato sauce
- 1 (16-ounce) can stewed tomatoes
- 3¼ cups chicken stock, heated
- 1 teaspoon salt
- ½ teaspoon MSG
- ½ teaspoon pepper

Sauté the rice in the butter in a saucepan until light brown. Stir in the onion, green pepper and garlic. Cook until the onion is tender, stirring constantly. Stir in the tomato sauce and undrained tomatoes. Cook until heated through, stirring frequently. Stir in the stock, salt, MSG and pepper. Cook, covered, over low heat for 20 minutes or until the rice is tender.

Makes 6 servings.

Kay Peck
San Antonio, Texas

Tip: *Eliminate unnecessary details. Example: Let dishes drain dry.*

*P*lease accept our humble family favorites. I wanted to participate in honor of my dad's memory and in some small way to thank Warm Springs for the wonderful care they gave him during his two stays. We will always be grateful!

Rita Ramirez Charles and Gloria Ramirez, daughters of former patient Richard Ramirez, San Antonio, Texas

Sausage Dressing

1	pound sausage
1	cup chopped celery
½	medium onion, chopped
½	green bell pepper, chopped
1	egg, beaten
1	package stuffing mix
2	cups water

*B*rown the sausage with the celery, onion and green pepper in a skillet, stirring until the sausage is crumbly; drain. Combine the sausage mixture, egg and stuffing mix in a large bowl and mix well. Add the water gradually, stirring until mixed. Spoon into a greased baking pan. Bake at 350 degrees for 35 to 40 minutes or until brown and bubbly. May use to stuff turkey. This recipe equals amount to be prepared per 5 pounds of turkey. Increase the ingredients according to size of turkey.

Makes 6 to 8 servings.

Gloria Ramirez
San Antonio, Texas

Baked Grits

1 cup grits
1 cup shredded sharp Cheddar cheese
1 roll garlic cheese, chopped
¼ cup butter, softened, chopped
1½ teaspoons Worcestershire sauce
  Salt to taste
  Red pepper to taste

Cook the grits using package directions. Stir in the Cheddar cheese, garlic cheese, butter, Worcestershire sauce, salt and red pepper. Spoon into a greased baking dish. Bake at 350 degrees for 30 minutes.

Makes 6 to 8 servings.

Bonnie Street
San Antonio, Texas

Jalapeño Rice

3 cups white rice
3 cups chicken broth
3 tablespoons butter
3 fresh jalapeños, roasted, peeled, seeded, chopped
3 cups sour cream
4½ cups shredded Monterey Jack cheese

Combine the rice, broth and butter in a saucepan. Bring to a boil; reduce heat. Cook, covered, over low heat for 25 minutes. Stir in the jalapeños. Spoon into a lightly buttered 3-quart baking dish. Spread the sour cream over the prepared layer. Sprinkle with the cheese. Bake at 350 degrees for 25 to 30 minutes or until the cheese melts. May substitute 3 tablespoons minced pickled jalapeños for the fresh jalapeños.

Makes 10 to 12 servings.

Linda Zealy
Victoria, Texas

Cherry Cheese Coffee Cake

1 (8-count) can crescent rolls
8 ounces cream cheese, softened
1/3 cup confectioners' sugar
1 egg
1/2 teaspoon vanilla extract
1 cup cherry pie filling
1/3 cup confectioners' sugar
2 teaspoons milk

Separate the crescent roll dough into triangles. Arrange the triangles in a circle with the points facing out on a baking sheet overlapping the edges to seal. Beat the cream cheese, 1/3 cup confectioners' sugar, egg and vanilla in a mixer bowl until smooth. Spread over the triangles; top with the pie filling. Twist each point and tuck into the middle. Bake at 350 degrees for 20 to 25 minutes or until golden brown. Drizzle with a mixture of 1/3 cup confectioners' sugar and milk.

Makes 8 to 10 servings.

Vicki Fisher
New Braunfels, Texas

Favorite Coffee Cake

3 cups flour
1 1/2 cups sugar
2 tablespoons baking powder
3/4 teaspoon salt
1 cup butter
2 eggs
1 cup milk
  Brown sugar
  Chopped nuts

Sift the flour, sugar, baking powder and salt into a bowl and mix well. Cut in the butter until crumbly. Beat the eggs in a bowl until pale yellow and fluffy. Fold in the flour mixture. Add the milk and mix well. Spoon the batter into 2 greased and floured 9-inch cake pans. Sprinkle generously with brown sugar and nuts. Bake at 325 degrees for 45 minutes.

Makes 10 to 12 servings.

Bonnie Street
San Antonio, Texas

Lakota Indian Fry Bread

- 4 cups self-rising flour
- 1 teaspoon baking powder
- 1/8 teaspoon salt
- 1 tablespoon shortening
- Vegetable oil for frying

Combine the flour, baking powder and salt in a bowl and mix well. Cut in the shortening until crumbly. Add just enough water to make an easily handled dough and mix well. Knead lightly. Let stand for several minutes. Shape into 1-inch or larger balls; flatten. Fry in hot oil in a skillet until brown on both sides; drain. Serve with honey, beans, soup or the dish of your choice. May be frozen for future use and reheated just before serving.

Makes variable servings.

David A. Wilson
Brownwood, Texas

Greek Bread

- 8 ounces mozzarella cheese, shredded
- 1 (4-ounce) can chopped black olives, drained
- 1 (4-ounce) can mushroom pieces, drained
- 1/2 cup margarine, softened
- 1/2 cup mayonnaise
- 4 green onions, chopped
- Garlic powder to taste
- 1 loaf French bread, split lengthwise into halves

Combine the cheese, black olives, mushrooms, margarine, mayonnaise, green onions and garlic powder in a bowl and mix well. Spread over the cut sides of the bread. Arrange cut side up on a baking sheet. Bake at 350 degrees for 20 minutes. Let stand for 15 minutes before slicing.

Makes 12 servings.

Michael Mahaffey
Corpus Christi, Texas

Old-Fashioned Walnut Bread

3	cups sifted flour
1	cup sugar
4	teaspoons baking powder
2	teaspoons salt
1½	cups milk
¼	cup melted shortening
1	egg, lightly beaten
1	teaspoon vanilla extract
2	cups chopped walnuts

Sift the flour, sugar, baking powder and salt into a bowl and mix well. Add the milk, shortening, egg and vanilla, stirring just until moistened. Fold in the walnuts. Spoon into a greased 5x9-inch loaf pan. Bake at 350 degrees for 1 hour and 20 minutes. May spoon the batter into 2 greased 29-ounce cans. Bake for 1 hour and 10 minutes or until the loaves test done.

Try these variations for a new twist: (1) Prepare the batter as above. Spoon ½ of the batter into a greased loaf pan. Sprinkle with a mixture of ⅓ cup packed brown sugar, 2 tablespoons butter, 1½ tablespoons flour and 1 teaspoon cinnamon. Top with the remaining batter. Bake as above. (2) Prepare the batter as above adding 2 teaspoons grated orange peel to the milk mixture. Fold in ¾ cup chopped candied fruit with the chopped walnuts. Bake as above.

Makes 1 loaf.

Donna Reichel
Katy, Texas

Pumpkin Bread

3½	cups sifted flour
3	cups sugar
2	teaspoons baking soda
1½	teaspoons salt
1	teaspoon cinnamon
1	teaspoon nutmeg
2	cups pumpkin
1	cup vegetable oil
⅔	cup water
4	eggs, beaten
1	teaspoon vanilla extract
1	cup chopped nuts

Combine the flour, sugar, baking soda, salt, cinnamon and nutmeg in a bowl and mix well. Stir in the pumpkin, oil, water, eggs and vanilla. Fold in the nuts. Spoon into 2 greased 5x9-inch loaf pans. Bake at 350 degrees for 1 hour or until the loaves test done.

Makes 2 loaves.

Louisa Mata
San Antonio, Texas

Morning Glory Muffins

2	cups flour
1¼	cups sugar
2	teaspoons baking soda
2	teaspoons cinnamon
½	teaspoon salt
2	cups grated carrots
½	cup raisins
½	cup shredded coconut
½	cup chopped pecans
1	cup vegetable oil
3	eggs
2	teaspoons vanilla extract

Combine the flour, sugar, baking soda, cinnamon and salt in a bowl and mix well. Stir in the carrots, raisins, coconut and pecans. Combine the oil, eggs and vanilla in a bowl and mix well. Add to the flour mixture gradually, stirring just until moistened. Spoon the batter into greased or paper-lined muffin cups. Bake at 350 degrees for 15 to 18 minutes or until the muffins test done.

Makes 18 muffins.

Barbara J. Cox
San Antonio, Texas

Being involved in Wheelchair Sports has given me more confidence in myself. It has made me feel excited about life, and it helps me reach my present goals.

David Scott Roberts, 1997 Junior Wheelchair Sports Athlete of the Year, San Antonio, Texas

Six-Week Muffins

1	(15-ounce) package Raisin Bran flakes
5	cups flour
3	cups sugar
5	teaspoons baking soda
1	teaspoon salt
4	cups buttermilk
4	eggs, lightly beaten
1	cup vegetable oil
	Chopped nuts
	Chopped dried fruit

Combine the cereal, flour, sugar, baking soda and salt in a bowl and mix well. Whisk the buttermilk and eggs together in a bowl. Add the buttermilk mixture and oil to the cereal mixture and mix well. Stir in chopped nuts, chopped dried fruit or any other desired ingredient. Fill paper-lined muffin cups 2/3 full. Bake at 350 degrees for 20 minutes or until the muffins test done. Store leftover batter in the refrigerator for up to 6 weeks. Use as desired.

Editor's Note: If batter is to be stored for a period of time, pasteurized egg substitute should be used instead of fresh eggs.

Makes 24 to 30 muffins.

Christine Sommers
San Antonio, Texas

Tip: *Chop dried fruit with kitchen shears dipped in hot water instead of using a knife.*

Success Is Opportunity — Warm Springs Resource Center

Throughout its 60-year history, Warm Springs has been known for continually responding to the changing needs of both adults and children with physical disabilities.

In response to the growing need for creative approaches to serve people with disabilities, the Warm Springs Foundation has recently undertaken a community project to develop and build a resource center. The primary goal of the center, to be constructed at Warm Springs+Baptist Rehabilitation Hospital in San Antonio, is to provide comprehensive programming to enhance the quality of life for people with disabilities, and to reduce and prevent disability through offering the following:

❖ Vocational Services: including vocational rehabilitation for disabled adults who are chronically unemployed, underemployed, or attempting to reenter the workforce. Services to employers, i.e. redesigning workplace features and job functions to enable the employment of disabled workers, will be incorporated.

❖ Recreation and Sports Activities: including an expanded Wheelchair Sports Program for children and adults; a Sports Medicine and Rehabilitation program for children and adults with mild, moderate, and severe injuries; and a therapeutic playground for ambulatory and non-ambulatory children.

❖ Education of the Body, Mind, and Spirit: including on-line training for homebound persons with disabilities, computer literacy and other adult education classes offered on-line and on-site, instruction and support in maintaining wellness, assisting people with disabilities to develop sufficient motivation for change and growth, a convening space for support groups, staff development via videoconferencing, and on-line and on-site opportunities for spiritual growth and renewal.

❖ Services to Special Populations: including a project to help disabled farmers and ranchers acquire assistive technology and new methods that will enable them to continue their livelihood and productivity. In addition, a full-service Motion Assessment Center to help determine the most appropriate surgeries or treatment for a wide range of conditions—orthopedic, spinal cord or brain injuries, Parkinson's Disease, cerebral palsy—with additional applications in prosthetic analysis, brace prescription, stability studies, and sports medicine.

The staff and board of the Warm Springs Rehabilitation Foundation have pledged to open the Resource Center in 1998; however, additional financial commitments from the community are necessary in order to complete the project. The Foundation is currently soliciting other partners interested in supporting the center.

For more information on how you or your company can help make the Warm Springs Resource Center project a reality, call the Warm Springs Foundation at 1-800-457-0777.

Desserts

The Warm Springs Resource Center will bring together a group of community partners to create Texas' first organized on-site and on-line comprehensive source of assistance, information, and educational opportunities especially for people with physical disabilities.

Apple Cake

- 2 cups grated apples
- 2 teaspoons baking soda
- 2 cups sugar
- 1 cup butter, softened
- 3 cups sifted flour
- 1 teaspoon cinnamon
- 1 teaspoon ground cloves (optional)
- 1 teaspoon nutmeg (optional)
- 1 teaspoon vanilla extract
- 1 cup raisins
- 1 cup chopped nuts

Combine the apples and baking soda in a bowl. Beat the sugar and butter in a mixer bowl until light and fluffy. Add the flour, cinnamon, cloves, nutmeg and vanilla and mix well. Stir in the apple mixture, raisins and nuts. Spoon into a bundt pan, 1 or 2 loaf pans or two 9-inch cake pans. Bake at 350 degrees until the cake tests done. Cool in pan for several minutes. Invert onto a wire rack to cool completely.

Makes 16 servings.

Cecilia N. Maresh
Moulton, Texas

Tip: *A whisk is easier to use for beating than a spoon because it offers less resistance. Choose one with a large handle for a comfortable grasp.*

*B*efore my accident, I took life for granted. But the accident opened new doors for me. It made me a responsible person, and I'm appreciating life a lot more.

Larry Quintero, 1996 Warm Springs Wheelchair Sports Adult Athlete of the Year, San Antonio, Texas

Apple Crunch Cake

2	cups sifted flour
2	cups sugar
1	teaspoon baking soda
1	teaspoon nutmeg
1	teaspoon cinnamon
½	teaspoon salt
1	cup vegetable oil
2	eggs
1	cup orange juice
2	cups chopped peeled apples
1	cup chopped pecans
1	teaspoon vanilla extract

Combine the flour, sugar, baking soda, nutmeg, cinnamon and salt in a bowl and mix well. Combine the oil and eggs in a bowl, beating until blended. Add the orange juice and mix well. Stir in the flour mixture. Fold in the apples, pecans and vanilla. Spoon into a greased and floured 9x13-inch cake pan. Bake at 350 degrees for 30 to 40 minutes or until the cake tests done. Invert onto a wire rack. Serve warm with ice cream. Do not allow the cake to cool in the pan.

Makes 15 servings.

Vannie Starr
San Antonio, Texas

Applesauce Fruitcake

2 cups applesauce
1 cup raisins
1 cup nuts
1 tablespoon melted butter
2 cups flour
1½ cups sugar
3 tablespoons cornstarch
2½ teaspoons baking cocoa
½ teaspoon salt
½ teaspoon allspice
½ teaspoon nutmeg
½ teaspoon cinnamon

Combine the applesauce, raisins, nuts and butter in a saucepan. Bring to a boil, stirring frequently. Remove from heat. Sift the flour, sugar, cornstarch, baking cocoa, salt, allspice, nutmeg and cinnamon into a bowl and mix well. Add to the applesauce mixture, stirring just until moistened. Spoon into a loaf pan. Bake at 350 degrees for 1 hour. Cool in pan for 10 minutes. Invert onto a wire rack to cool completely.

Makes 12 servings.

Submitted by Denise E. Robinson in memory of Isaac L. Robinson San Antonio, Texas

Tip: *When stirring, use the whole arm–freeze the wrist and use the elbow and shoulder.*

*T*hrough all these years, Warm Springs has remained on the forefront while never losing sight of what matters most–patient care. Before making any decision, Warm Springs has always asked, "What will this do for the patient?"

Esther Bell, longtime occupational therapist and quality/standards director (retired), Gonzales, Texas

Applesauce Spice Cake

2	cups sifted flour
1	cup sugar
2	teaspoons baking soda
1	teaspoon allspice
1	teaspoon ground cloves
1	teaspoon cinnamon
½	teaspoon salt
1	(4-ounce) jar maraschino cherries, drained
1	cup chopped dates
1	cup chopped raisins
1	cup chopped nuts
1½	cups canned applesauce, chilled
½	cup melted butter or shortening
1	teaspoon vanilla extract

*S*ift the flour, sugar, baking soda, allspice, cloves, cinnamon and salt into a bowl and mix well. Stir in the maraschino cherries, dates, raisins and nuts. Add the applesauce, butter and vanilla, stirring until mixed. Spoon into a loaf pan or tube pan. Bake at 350 degrees for 1 hour or until the cake tests done. Cool in pan for several minutes. Invert onto a wire rack to cool completely. May sprinkle with whole maraschino cherries and/or pecan halves before baking if desired.

Makes 16 servings.

Ophelia Brown
Boerne, Texas

Apricot Nectar Cake

- 1 (2-layer) package yellow cake mix
- 1 small package lemon gelatin or pudding mix
- 1 cup apricot nectar
- ¾ cup vegetable oil
- 4 eggs
- 1 teaspoon vanilla extract
- 1 cup sifted confectioners' sugar
  Lemon juice to taste

Combine the cake mix and gelatin in a mixer bowl and mix well. Add the apricot nectar and oil. Beat for 4 to 5 minutes, scraping the bowl occasionally. Add the eggs 1 at a time, beating well after each addition. Beat in the vanilla. Spoon into a greased and floured tube pan. Bake at 325 degrees for 1 hour or until the cake tests done. Cool in the pan for 10 minutes. Invert onto a wire rack to cool completely. Combine the confectioners' sugar and lemon juice in a small bowl, stirring until of glaze consistency. Drizzle over the cake.

Makes 16 servings.

Isabelle J. Hall
Lubbock, Texas

Banana Cake

1	(2-layer) package yellow cake mix
1	(4-ounce) package banana cream instant pudding mix
½	cup vegetable oil
½	cup water
2	eggs
3	very ripe bananas, mashed
1	cup confectioners' sugar, sifted
2	tablespoons (about) water

Combine the cake mix, pudding mix, oil, water and eggs in a large bowl and mix until smooth and creamy. Add the bananas and mix well. Pour into a greased and floured bundt pan. Bake at 350 degrees for 40 minutes or until the cake tests done. Cool in the pan on a wire rack for 10 minutes. Invert onto a cake plate. Blend the confectioners' sugar with enough water to make a mixture of drizzling consistency. Drizzle the glaze over the warm cake. Let stand until cooled completely.

Makes 16 servings.

Scarlett O'Neill
Yoakum, Texas

Anytime someone tells me I can't do something, I just have to try harder to do it because there is a way. You just have to figure it out on your own. If someone isn't willing to help you, then you just have to come up with your own method.

Vanessa Vance, Warm Springs Wheelchair Sports participant, San Antonio, Texas

Blueberry Banana Snack Cake

- 1¼ cups sugar
- ⅔ cup melted butter or margarine
- ¼ cup buttermilk
- 2 eggs
- 1 teaspoon vanilla extract
- 2 cups mashed bananas
- 2 cups flour
- ¾ teaspoon baking soda
- ⅛ teaspoon salt
- 1 cup fresh or frozen blueberries
  Confectioners' sugar

Combine the sugar, butter, buttermilk, eggs and vanilla in a mixer bowl. Beat at medium speed for 1 to 2 minutes or until creamy, scraping the bowl frequently. Add the bananas. Beat for 1 minute or until blended. Add the flour, baking soda and salt. Beat at low speed for 1 to 2 minutes or just until moistened. Stir in the blueberries. Spoon into an 11x13-inch cake pan. Bake at 350 degrees for 25 to 30 minutes or until the cake tests done. Invert onto a wire rack to cool. Sprinkle with confectioners' sugar just before serving. May substitute a mixture of 1 teaspoon lemon juice or vinegar with enough milk to equal ¼ cup for the buttermilk.

Makes 16 servings.

Verna Mae Rodgers
Wrightsboro, Texas

Old-Fashioned Banana Cake

- 1 (2-layer) package yellow cake mix
- 1½ cups mashed bananas
- ½ cup water
- ¼ cup vegetable oil
- ¾ teaspoon baking powder
- 3 eggs or ¾ cup egg substitute
- ½ cup chopped pecans
- ¼ cup butter or margarine, softened
- ½ cup sugar
- ½ cup flour

Combine the cake mix, bananas, water, oil, baking powder and eggs in a bowl and mix well. Stir in the pecans. Spoon into a greased and floured 9x13-inch cake pan. Combine the butter, sugar and flour in a bowl, stirring until crumbly. Sprinkle over the prepared layer. Bake at 350 degrees for 40 minutes or until brown and the cake tests done. Serve warm or cold but the cake is best when served warm.

Makes 15 servings.

Betty Schmidt
La Grange, Texas

Gingerbread

- 2 cups sifted flour
- 1½ teaspoons ground ginger
- 1½ teaspoons baking powder
- 1 teaspoon salt
- ¾ teaspoon baking soda
- ½ teaspoon ground cloves
- ¾ cup molasses
- ⅔ cup boiling water
- ½ cup shortening
- ½ cup sugar
- 1 egg

Sift the flour, ginger, baking powder, salt, baking soda and cloves into a mixer bowl and mix well. Add the molasses, boiling water, shortening, sugar and egg. Beat at low speed for 1 minute. Spoon into a greased and floured 5x9-inch loaf pan. Bake at 350 degrees for 40 minutes. Cool in the pan for several minutes. Invert onto a wire rack to cool completely.

Makes 12 servings.

Debra Clark
Toronto, Canada

Best-Ever Chocolate Cake

2	cups flour
2	cups sugar
½	cup baking cocoa
1	teaspoon baking soda
½	teaspoon salt
2	eggs
1	cup vegetable oil
1	cup buttermilk
1	cup boiling water
1	teaspoon vanilla extract
	Chocolate Frosting

Combine the flour, sugar, baking cocoa, baking soda and salt in a bowl and mix well. Add the eggs, oil and buttermilk and mix well. Stir in the boiling water and vanilla. Spoon into a greased and floured 9x13-inch cake pan. Bake at 350 degrees for 20 to 30 minutes or until the cake tests done. Spread the hot Chocolate Frosting over the warm cake.

Makes 15 servings.

Chocolate Frosting

1	cup sugar
1	cup water
3	tablespoons cornstarch
2	tablespoons baking cocoa
2	tablespoons margarine
1	teaspoon vanilla extract

Combine the sugar, water, cornstarch and baking cocoa in a saucepan and mix well. Cook over medium heat until thickened, stirring constantly. Stir in the margarine and vanilla.

Jennifer Malatek
Gonzales, Texas

Lemon Cake

- 1 (2-layer) package yellow cake mix
- 1 (3-ounce) package lemon gelatin
- 4 eggs
- ¾ cup water
- ¾ cup vegetable oil
  Lemon Glaze

Combine the cake mix and gelatin in a mixer bowl and mix well. Add the eggs 1 at a time, beating well after each addition. Add the water. Beat for 2 minutes, scraping the bowl occasionally. Add the oil. Beat for 1 minute. Spoon into a greased and floured 9x13-inch cake pan. Bake at 350 degrees for 35 to 40 minutes or until the cake tests done. Pierce the top of the cake with a fork, pushing the tines through the layer. Drizzle with the Lemon Glaze.

Makes 12 servings.

Lemon Glaze

- 2 cups confectioners' sugar
  Juice of 2 lemons
  Grated peel of 1 lemon

Combine the confectioners' sugar, lemon juice and lemon peel in a bowl, stirring until of a glaze consistency.

Bonnie S. Buchholtz
Gonzales, Texas

I could sit around and dwell on ifs and should-have-beens all day, but I realized that what happened happened, and I have to go on. I was lucky that Warm Springs was there for me.

Chris Hessler, former spinal-cord-injury patient, Victoria, Texas

Orange Cake

2 3/4   cups cake flour
1 1/2   cups sugar
1 1/2   cups buttermilk, at room temperature
1/2   cup butter or margarine, softened
1/4   cup shortening
3   eggs, at room temperature
1   tablespoon grated orange peel
1 1/2   teaspoons baking soda
1 1/2   teaspoons vanilla extract
3/4   teaspoon salt
1   cup chopped golden raisins
1/2   cup finely chopped nuts
    Butter Frosting

Combine the cake flour, sugar, buttermilk, butter, shortening, eggs, orange peel, baking soda, vanilla and salt in a mixer bowl. Beat at low speed for 30 seconds, scraping the bowl constantly. Beat at high speed for 3 minutes, scraping the bowl occasionally. Stir in the raisins and nuts. Spoon into 3 greased and floured 8-inch cake pans. Bake at 350 degrees for 30 to 35 minutes or until the layers test done. Invert onto a wire rack to cool. Spread the Butter Frosting between the layers and over the top and side of the cake. May substitute 2 1/2 cups all-purpose flour for the cake flour. The flavor is enhanced if this cake is prepared several days before serving.

Makes 12 servings.

Butter Frosting

4 1/2   cups confectioners' sugar
1/2   cup butter or margarine, softened
4   to 5 teaspoons orange-flavor liqueur or orange juice
1   tablespoon grated orange peel

Beat the confectioners' sugar and butter in a mixer bowl until smooth, scraping the bowl occasionally. Add the liqueur and orange peel. Beat until of a spreading consistency, scraping the bowl frequently.

Emma Blakeway
Houston, Texas

It was so exhilarating, and so many people saw me on TV. I just wanted to scream "Look at me! Look at me!"

Diana Vradenburg, former joint-replacement patient and ALLCANSKI adapted waterski participant, New Braunfels, Texas

Orange Christmas Cake

4	cups sifted flour
1	teaspoon baking soda
2	cups sugar
1	cup butter or shortening
4	eggs, beaten
1½	cups buttermilk
1	teaspoon vanilla extract
4	cups finely chopped pecans
16	ounces orange candy slices, finely chopped
2	cups packed brown sugar
1	cup orange juice

Mix the flour and baking soda. Beat the sugar and butter in a mixer bowl until light and fluffy. Add the eggs and mix well. Add the flour mixture and buttermilk alternately, beating well after each addition. Stir in the vanilla, pecans and candy. Spoon into a cake pan. Bake at 275 degrees for 1½ to 2 hours or until the cake tests done. Combine the brown sugar and orange juice in a saucepan. Cook over low heat until blended, stirring frequently. Let stand until cool. Pour over the warm cake. May freeze for future use.

Makes 15 servings.

*Theresa Meitzen
Cuero, Texas*

Pineapple Upside-Down Cake

1	cup plus 2 tablespoons flour
1	teaspoon baking powder
1	cup packed brown sugar
1/3	cup butter
5	slices pineapple
1/2	cup chopped nuts
3	egg yolks
1	cup sugar
1/2	cup pineapple juice
1	teaspoon vanilla extract
3	egg whites, stiffly beaten

Sift the flour and baking powder together and set aside. Combine the brown sugar and butter in a cast-iron skillet. Heat the brown sugar mixture over low heat until melted. Arrange the pineapple slices in the skillet and sprinkle with the nuts. Cook over very low heat while preparing the cake batter. Beat the egg yolks in a large bowl. Add the sugar, pineapple juice and vanilla and mix well. Add the flour mixture and mix until smooth. Fold in the stiffly beaten egg whites gently. Pour the batter into the prepared skillet. Bake at 350 degrees for 25 to 30 minutes or until the cake tests done. Invert the cake onto a serving platter immediately. Serve the cake plain or with whipped cream or whipped topping.

Makes 6 to 8 servings.

Marguerite Bohne
Cuero, Texas

I resided at Gonzales Warm Springs Rehabilitation Hospital from September until November 1981. I am still wheelchair bound, but I love to bake and cook. I suppose you could call it my favorite pastime since other activities for me are limited. I think this is a great idea to publish a cookbook.

*Barbara Cox, former patient,
San Antonio, Texas*

Pineapple Cake

2	cups flour
1 1/2	cups sugar
1	teaspoon baking soda
1/8	teaspoon salt
1	(20-ounce) can crushed pineapple
2	eggs
1/2	cup packed brown sugar
	Chopped pecans
1	cup milk
3/4	cup sugar
1/2	cup margarine
1	teaspoon vanilla extract

Combine the flour, 1 1/2 cups sugar, baking soda and salt in a bowl and mix well. Stir in the undrained pineapple and eggs. Spoon into a greased and floured 9x13-inch cake pan. Sprinkle with a mixture of the brown sugar and pecans. Bake at 350 degrees for 30 minutes. Cool slightly. Bring the milk, 3/4 cup sugar and margarine to a boil in a saucepan. Stir in the vanilla. Pour over the warm cake.

Makes 16 servings.

*Karen Hayden
Lubbock, Texas*

Rum Cake

- 1 cup chopped pecans
- 1 (2-layer) package butter cake mix
- ½ cup corn oil
- 1 (4-ounce) package vanilla instant pudding mix
- ½ cup cold water
- ½ cup dark rum
- Rum Glaze

Grease and flour a bundt pan. Sprinkle the pecans over the bottom and side of the pan. Combine the cake mix, corn oil, pudding mix, cold water and rum in a mixer bowl and beat until smooth. Spoon into the prepared pan. Bake at 325 degrees for 1 hour or until the cake tests done. Pour the Rum Glaze over the cake and down the side. Let stand for 15 minutes. Invert onto a cake plate; do not remove the pan until the cake is cool.

Makes 24 servings.

Rum Glaze

- 1 cup sugar
- ½ cup butter
- ¼ cup water
- ½ cup dark rum

Combine the sugar, butter and water in a saucepan. Bring to a boil. Boil for 5 minutes, stirring occasionally. Remove from heat. Stir in the rum.

Beverly Anderson
Columbus, Texas

Strawberry Cake

1   (2-layer) package white cake mix
1   envelope whipped topping mix
1   (3-ounce) package strawberry gelatin
1   cup vegetable oil
½   cup water
4   eggs
½   package frozen sliced strawberries
    Strawberry Frosting

Combine the cake mix, whipped topping mix, strawberry gelatin, oil, water and eggs in a bowl and mix well. Fold in the strawberries. Spoon into a 10x15-inch cake pan. Bake at 350 degrees for 25 to 30 minutes or until the cake tests done. Cool in the pan on a wire rack. Spread with the Strawberry Frosting.
    Makes 16 servings.

Strawberry Frosting

1   (1-pound) package confectioners' sugar
4   ounces cream cheese, softened
¼   cup butter, softened
½   package frozen sliced strawberries, thawed
1   cup chopped pecans (optional)

Beat the confectioners' sugar, cream cheese and butter in a mixer bowl until creamy. Fold in the strawberries and pecans.

Carolyn Buschfort
San Antonio, Texas

Shawna Chumchal
Shiner, Texas

One of my fondest memories involves a seventeen-year-old patient who had spent his whole life lying flat on his back looking up toward the walls or ceiling. After being fitted for a special padded insert, he was put into a new manual wheelchair and later a powered wheelchair. It was very moving because his first comment was "So that's how things are supposed to look!"

George Christian, longtime Warm Springs orthotist, deceased

Texas Vanilla Sheet Cake

2 2/3 cups flour
2 cups sugar
1 cup water
1/2 cup margarine
1/2 cup vegetable oil
2/3 cup buttermilk
2 eggs, beaten
2 teaspoons vanilla extract
1 teaspoon baking soda
    Cinnamon to taste
    Cream Cheese Frosting
    Chopped nuts (optional)

Combine the flour and sugar in a bowl and mix well. Combine the water, margarine and oil in a saucepan. Bring to a boil. Pour over the flour mixture, beating with a whisk or wooden spoon until blended. Stir in the buttermilk, eggs, vanilla, baking soda and cinnamon. Spoon into a greased 10x15-inch cake pan. Bake at 350 degrees for 25 minutes. Cool in pan on wire rack just until warm. Spread with the Cream Cheese Frosting. Let stand until set. Sprinkle with the chopped nuts.

    Makes 24 servings.

Tip: *Push or roll objects instead of lifting them.*

Cream Cheese Frosting

8 ounces cream cheese, softened
1/2 cup margarine, softened
1 teaspoon vanilla extract

Combine the cream cheese, margarine and vanilla in a mixer bowl. Beat until of spreading consistency, scraping the bowl frequently.

Kathy Jurek
Gonzales, Texas

Divinity

3   cups sugar
1   cup water
3   tablespoons corn syrup
2   egg whites
    Vanilla extract to taste
    Chopped nuts

Combine the sugar, water and corn syrup in a saucepan. Cook over medium heat to 234 to 240 degrees on a candy thermometer, soft-ball stage. Remove from heat. Let stand until cool. Beat the egg whites in a mixer bowl until stiff peaks form. Pour the cooled sugar syrup gradually into the egg whites. Beat for 30 minutes or until shiny. Fold in the vanilla and nuts. Drop by spoonfuls onto waxed paper or a buttered baking sheet.

Makes 1 1/2 pounds.

Bonnie Street
San Antonio, Texas

Pinto Bean Fiesta Fudge

1   cup warm cooked pinto beans
3/4 cup melted butter
1   cup baking cocoa
1   tablespoon vanilla extract
2   (1-pound) packages confectioners' sugar
1   cup chopped pecans

Mash the beans in a bowl. Add the butter, baking cocoa and vanilla and mix well. Add the confectioners' sugar gradually, stirring until mixed. Stir in the pecans. Press into a buttered 9x13-inch dish. Chill until set.

Makes 36 to 48 servings.

Linda Lee Davis
San Antonio, Texas

Microwave Peanut Brittle

1   cup sugar
1   cup raw peanuts
1/2 cup light corn syrup
1   teaspoon butter
1   teaspoon vanilla extract
1   teaspoon baking soda

Combine the sugar, peanuts and corn syrup in a microwave-safe dish. Microwave on High for 4 minutes; stir. Microwave for 4 minutes; stir. Add the butter and mix well. Microwave for 2 minutes; stir. Add the vanilla and mix well. Microwave for several seconds or until the mixture is light brown. Stir in the baking soda. Spread evenly on a greased baking sheet. Let stand until cool. Break into pieces. Store in an airtight container.

Makes variable servings.

Onie Baker
Gonzales, Texas

Belgian Almond Cookies

2	cups butter or margarine, softened
2	cups sugar
1	tablespoon almond extract
1	teaspoon vanilla extract
4	egg yolks
5 1/3	cups sifted cake flour
1 1/2	cups chopped blanched almonds
1	teaspoon salt
36	whole almonds
4	egg whites, lightly beaten

Beat the butter in a mixer bowl until creamy. Add the sugar and flavorings. Beat until light and fluffy, scraping the bowl occasionally. Add the egg yolks 1 at a time, beating well after each addition. Stir in the cake flour, chopped almonds and salt. Shape into small balls. Arrange on a greased cookie sheet. Flatten each ball. Dip the whole almonds in the egg whites. Top each cookie with an almond. Bake at 350 degrees for 10 to 14 minutes or until light golden brown. Remove to a wire rack to cool.

Makes 3 dozen cookies.

Margarita Hinojosa
Corpus Christi, Texas

Black-Skillet Brownies

½   cup margarine
1   cup packed brown sugar
1   cup flour
½   to ¾ cup chopped pecans
1   egg, lightly beaten
1   teaspoon baking powder
½   teaspoon vanilla extract
⅛   teaspoon salt
6   scoops vanilla ice cream

Heat the margarine in an 8- or 9-inch black cast-iron skillet until melted. Stir in the brown sugar, flour, pecans, egg, baking powder, vanilla and salt. Bake in the skillet at 350 degrees for 20 minutes. Cool slightly. Cut into wedges. Top each wedge with a scoop of vanilla ice cream.

Makes 6 servings.

Linda Zealy
Victoria, Texas

Born in 1952 on a small farm near Kenedy, Texas, Deana Voges contracted polio at the age of six months. First entering Gonzales Warm Springs Rehabilitation Hospital when she was ten months old, Deana spent a total of four out of the first six years of her life there.

While challenged by partial paralysis, Voges pressed on through high school and Texas A & I University before receiving a master of divinity degree at Lutheran Theological Southern Seminary in Columbus, South Carolina.

Today, she's serving her seventh year as a Warm Springs chaplain, offering a sense of love, worth, hope, and faith to staff, patients, and their families. Many years after being a pediatric polio patient, she maintains that her service with Warm Springs is like going home.

"There's a history here, not just the people or the place, but the memories of recovery. My mission now is to make people know that they're worthwhile, regardless of what their physical bodies can or cannot do. Their spirit is still there, and that's what counts."

Blarney Kisses

1	cup sugar
½	cup butter or margarine, softened
2	eggs
1	teaspoon vanilla extract
2	ounces unsweetened chocolate, melted
½	cup flour
½	cup chopped walnuts
	Mint Frosting
1	ounce unsweetened chocolate
1	tablespoon butter

Beat the sugar and ½ cup butter in a mixer bowl until light and fluffy. Add the eggs and vanilla, beating until blended. Stir in the melted chocolate. Add the flour and walnuts and mix well. Spoon into an 8x8-inch baking pan. Bake at 350 degrees for 25 minutes. Cool in the pan on a wire rack. Spread with the Mint Frosting. Heat 1 ounce chocolate and 1 tablespoon butter in a saucepan, stirring until blended. Cool slightly. Pour over the prepared layers, tilting the pan to cover evenly. Let stand until set. Cut into ¾x2-inch bars.

Makes 40 bars.

Tip: *Use a pizza cutter to slice bar cookies.*

Mint Frosting

1	cup confectioners' sugar
2	tablespoons butter or margarine, softened
1	tablespoon light cream or milk
½	teaspoon peppermint extract
1	drop (about) of green food coloring

Combine the confectioners' sugar, butter, cream, peppermint extract and food coloring in a mixer bowl. Beat until of spreading consistency, scraping the bowl occasionally.

Erin Johnson
Fort Worth, Texas

It takes special people, children of God, to be able to go through this with people like me and others who are in much worse shape than I. But the nurses, therapists, and others are so patient. Through all of this we just keep on trying.

Carl Grothe, former spinal-cord-injury patient, Cameron, Texas

Crunchy Nut Cookies

1	cup sifted flour
1	teaspoon baking soda
½	teaspoon salt
1	cup sugar
1	cup packed brown sugar
½	cup shortening
2	eggs
1	teaspoon vanilla extract
1	cup chopped nuts

Sift the flour, baking soda and salt together. Beat the sugar, brown sugar, shortening, eggs and vanilla in a mixer bowl until light and fluffy. Stir in the flour mixture. Add the nuts and mix well. Shape the dough into balls. Arrange on an ungreased cookie sheet; flatten with the bottom of a greased glass. Bake at 375 degrees for 8 to 10 minutes or until light brown. Remove to a wire rack to cool.

Makes 5 dozen cookies.

Theresa Meitzen
Cuero, Texas

Macadamia Nut and White Chocolate Cookies

½	cup margarine, softened
½	cup shortening
¾	cup packed light brown sugar
½	cup sugar
1	egg
1½	teaspoons vanilla extract
2	cups flour
1	teaspoon baking soda
⅛	teaspoon salt
6	ounces white chocolate, broken into pieces
7	ounces macadamia nuts, chopped

Beat the margarine and shortening in a mixer bowl until creamy. Add the brown sugar and sugar, beating until light and fluffy. Beat in the egg and vanilla. Combine the flour, baking soda and salt in a bowl and mix well. Add to the creamed mixture, beating until blended. Stir in the white chocolate and macadamia nuts. Drop by spoonfuls onto a greased cookie sheet. Bake at 325 degrees just until light brown. Remove to a wire rack to cool.

Makes 3 dozen cookies.

Myrtle Colwell
Nixon, Texas

Cheater Cookies

11	graham crackers, split into halves
1/2	cup butter
1/2	cup sugar
6	tablespoons margarine
3/4	cup pecan pieces

Arrange the graham crackers in a single layer on a cookie sheet. Combine the butter, sugar and margarine in a saucepan. Bring to a boil. Boil for 3 minutes, stirring occasionally. Pour over the graham crackers; sprinkle with the pecans. Bake at 350 degrees for 10 minutes. Remove the cookies with a spatula to a sheet of foil immediately. Let stand until cool. May use chocolate graham crackers.

Makes 22 cookies.

Jenny Blair
Lakehills, Texas

Forgotten Cookies

2	egg whites
3/4	cup sugar
1	teaspoon vanilla extract
1	cup chocolate chips
1	cup chopped pecans

Preheat the oven to 325 degrees. Beat the egg whites in a large bowl until very stiff and dry peaks form. Fold in the sugar and vanilla gently. Fold in the chocolate chips and pecans. Drop the batter by teaspoonfuls onto a foil-covered cookie sheet. Place the cookie sheet in the preheated oven. Turn off the oven. Let the cookies stand in the closed oven for 6 to 8 hours; do not open the oven door. Remove from the oven and peel off the foil. Store the cookies in an airtight container.

Makes 36 cookies.

Mildred Hays
San Antonio, Texas

Warm Springs has been successful because of its spirit, great health care professionals, and fine management—making it simply the best.

Lynn Smith Jr., former Foundation board member, Gonzales, Texas

Millionaire Squares

1	(2-layer) package yellow cake mix
½	cup melted margarine
1	egg, beaten
1	cup chopped pecans
1	(1-pound) package confectioners' sugar
8	ounces cream cheese, softened
2	eggs
1	teaspoon vanilla extract

Combine the cake mix, margarine and 1 egg in a bowl and mix well. Stir in the pecans. Press into a greased and floured 9x13-inch baking pan. Beat the confectioners' sugar, cream cheese, 2 eggs and vanilla in a mixer bowl until smooth, scraping the bowl occasionally. Spread over the prepared layer. Bake at 350 degrees for 10 minutes. Reduce the oven temperature to 325 degrees. Bake for 45 minutes longer. Let stand until cool. Cut into squares.

Makes 24 squares.

Margaret Favor
Pleasanton, Texas

Wheelchair Sports has given me the opportunity to compete with others. It has enabled me to encourage other disabled athletes to participate and overcome their physical disabilities and succeed in every aspect of life.

Gilbert Garcia, 1997 Wheelchair Sports Adult Athlete of the Year, San Antonio, Texas

Favorite Oatmeal Cookies

5	cups rolled oats
2	cups butter, softened
2	cups sugar
2	cups packed brown sugar
4	eggs
2	teaspoons vanilla extract
4	cups flour
2	teaspoons baking powder
2	teaspoons baking soda
1	teaspoon salt
4	cups chocolate chips
1	(8-ounce) chocolate candy bar, grated
3	cups chopped nuts

Process the oats in a blender until powdery. Beat the butter, sugar and brown sugar in a mixer bowl until light and fluffy, scraping the bowl occasionally. Add the eggs and vanilla and mix well. Combine the blended oats, flour, baking powder, baking soda and salt in a bowl and mix well. Add to the creamed mixture, beating until blended. Stir in the chocolate chips, candy bar and nuts. Shape into 1-inch balls. Arrange 2 inches apart on a cookie sheet. Bake at 375 degrees for 10 minutes. Remove to a wire rack to cool. This recipe may be halved.

Makes 112 cookies.

Frank Sancho
San Antonio, Texas

Teacakes

- ½ cup butter or margarine, softened
- 1 cup sugar
- 2 eggs
- 1 teaspoon vanilla extract
- 1 tablespoon milk
- 2¼ cups flour
- 2 teaspoons baking powder

Cream the butter and sugar in a large bowl until light and fluffy. Add the eggs, vanilla and milk and mix until smooth. Mix the flour and baking powder together. Add to the creamed mixture and mix well. Shape the dough into 12 large balls with floured hands. Flatten each ball into a circle and arrange on a greased cookie sheet with the edges touching slightly. Bake at 400 degrees until light brown. Cool on the cookie sheet for 1 to 2 minutes. Remove to a wire rack to cool completely.

Makes 12 large cookies.

Valerie Tew
Jonesboro, Louisiana

Orange Slice Bars

4	eggs
2¼	cups packed brown sugar
2	cups flour
½	teaspoon salt
1	cup chopped pecans
14	orange candy slices, chopped

Beat the eggs in a mixer bowl until frothy. Add the brown sugar, beating until blended. Beat in the flour and salt. Stir in the pecans and chopped orange slices; batter will be thick. Spread in a greased and floured cookie sheet. Bake at 350 degrees for 25 minutes. Cut into bars immediately. Cool in pan.

Makes 32 bars.

Addie M. Pratt
Waelder, Texas

World's Best Cookies

1	cup margarine, softened
1	cup sugar
1	cup packed brown sugar
1	egg
1	cup vegetable oil
1	teaspoon vanilla extract
1	cup rolled oats
1	cup crushed cornflakes
½	cup shredded coconut
½	cup chopped pecans
3½	cups flour
1	teaspoon baking soda
1	teaspoon salt
	Sugar

Beat the margarine, 1 cup sugar and brown sugar in a mixer bowl until creamy, scraping the bowl occasionally. Add the egg and oil and beat well. Stir in the vanilla. Add the oats, cornflakes, coconut and pecans, stirring until mixed. Stir in a mixture of the flour, baking soda and salt. Shape into 1-inch balls. Arrange on an ungreased cookie sheet. Flatten each ball with a fork dipped in water. Bake at 350 degrees for 12 minutes. Sprinkle with sugar. Remove to a wire rack to cool.

Makes 8 dozen cookies.

Mildred Jarvis
Victoria, Texas

Caramel Crunch Apple Pie

4	cups sliced peeled apples
1	unbaked (9-inch) pie shell
24	caramels
2	tablespoons water
¾	cup flour
⅓	cup sugar
½	teaspoon cinnamon
⅓	cup margarine
½	cup chopped walnuts

Arrange the apples in the pie shell. Combine the caramels and water in a saucepan. Cook over low heat until smooth, stirring frequently. Pour over the apples. Combine the flour, sugar and cinnamon in a bowl and mix well. Cut in the margarine until crumbly. Stir in the walnuts. Sprinkle over the prepared layers. Bake at 375 degrees for 40 to 45 minutes or until the apples are tender.
   Makes 8 servings.

Lorine M. Dierschke
Moulton, Texas

Tip: *Use a knife like a dagger and pull it toward you instead of sawing with it.*

Coconut Cream Pie

1	unbaked (10-inch) deep-dish pie shell
2¾	cups milk
½	teaspoon coconut extract
1	(6-ounce) package vanilla instant pudding mix
1	cup flaked coconut
8	ounces whipped topping

Bake the pie shell using package directions. Let stand until cool. Combine the milk and coconut extract in a mixer bowl and mix well. Add the pudding mix. Beat for 2 minutes. Stir in the coconut gently. Pour into the pie shell. Spread with the whipped topping. Chill until serving time.

Makes 8 servings.

Janice P. Gates
San Antonio, Texas

Tip: When using a rolling pin, place your hands on top of the rolling pin rather than on the handles.

Crustless Coconut Pie

2	cups milk
1¾	cups sugar
½	cup flour
¼	cup melted margarine
4	eggs, lightly beaten
½	teaspoon baking powder
¼	teaspoon salt
1	(4-ounce) can shredded coconut
1	teaspoon vanilla extract

Combine the milk, sugar, flour, margarine, eggs, baking powder and salt in a bowl and mix well. Stir in the coconut and vanilla. Pour into a buttered 9-inch pie plate. Bake at 350 degrees for 40 to 45 minutes.

Makes 8 servings.

Evelyn Mutschler
Smiley, Texas

Impossible Pie

2	cups milk
4	eggs
½	cup flour
¼	cup margarine, softened
1	cup sugar
¼	teaspoon salt
¼	teaspoon nutmeg
1	teaspoon vanilla extract
1	to 2 cups shredded coconut (optional)

Combine the milk, eggs, flour, margarine, sugar, salt, nutmeg and vanilla in a blender container. Process for 1 minute or until well mixed. Mix in the coconut. Pour into a greased and floured 10-inch glass pie plate. Bake at 350 degrees for 45 minutes or until a knife inserted in the center comes out clean. Cool on a wire rack.

Makes 6 servings.

Mildred Hays
San Antonio, Texas

Lemon Pie

1   (14-ounce) can sweetened condensed milk
12 ounces whipped topping
1   (6-ounce) can frozen lemonade concentrate, thawed
1   baked (9-inch) pie shell

Blend the condensed milk and whipped topping in a bowl. Add the lemonade concentrate and blend well. Pour the mixture into the cooled pie shell. Chill the pie until serving time and the filling is firm.

Makes 6 servings.

Mildred Hays
San Antonio, Texas

Pinto Bean Pie

1   cup mashed pinto beans, heated
1   cup sugar
½   cup cream
2   tablespoons flour
1   tablespoon melted butter
½   teaspoon cinnamon
½   teaspoon ground cloves
½   teaspoon allspice
1   unbaked (9-inch) pie shell

Combine the pinto beans, sugar, cream, flour, butter, cinnamon, cloves and allspice in a bowl and mix well. Spoon into the pie shell. Bake at 350 degrees for 15 to 25 minutes or until light brown.

Makes 6 to 8 servings.

Arthur B. McKinney
Luling, Texas

Pumpkin Pie

- 1 (9-inch) graham cracker pie shell
- 1 (16-ounce) can pumpkin
- 1 cup plain low-fat yogurt
- 1/4 cup packed brown sugar
- 1 egg, beaten
- 1 teaspoon cinnamon or pumpkin pie spice (optional)

Bake the pie shell at 375 degrees for 10 minutes. Combine the pumpkin and yogurt in a bowl and mix well. Stir in the brown sugar, egg and cinnamon. Spoon into the baked pie shell. Place on a baking sheet. Bake at 400 degrees for 1 hour. Cool on a wire rack for 1 hour. Chill for several hours before serving to enhance flavor.
Makes 6 servings.

Jack Pirson
Austin, Texas

Strawberry Pie

- 1 cup sugar
- 2 tablespoons cornstarch
- 1/4 cup strawberry gelatin
- 1 cup hot water
- 1 to 2 pints fresh strawberries, hulled
- 1 baked (9-inch) pie shell
- 8 ounces whipped topping

Combine the sugar, cornstarch and gelatin in a saucepan and mix well. Stir in the hot water. Bring to a boil, stirring until the sugar and gelatin dissolve. Boil for 2 minutes or until the mixture coats the spoon. Arrange the strawberries in the cooled pie shell. Drizzle the syrup over the strawberries. Chill the pie until serving time. Top with whipped topping before serving.
Makes 6 to 8 servings.

Carolyn Buschfort
San Antonio, Texas

I didn't want to go through this, but when I look back, I realize I could not have gotten through it without the tremendous support of the Warm Springs staff, my family and friends, Texas A&M supporters, and the others who were in therapy with me.

Toby Boenig, former spinal-cord injury patient, Marion, Texas

English Toffee Pie

1	cup sugar
3/4	cup butter, softened
3	(1-ounce) packages melted chocolate
1 1/2	teaspoons vanilla extract
1 1/2	teaspoons instant coffee
3	eggs
	Toffee Pie Crust
1	cup whipping cream, whipped
1	tablespoon crumb mixture (reserved from Toffee Pie Crust)

Beat the sugar and butter in a mixer bowl until creamy. Add the chocolate, vanilla and coffee, beating until blended. Add the eggs 1 at a time, beating for 2 minutes after each addition. Spoon into the Toffee Pie Crust. Chill for 2 to 4 hours or until set. Spread with the whipped cream. Sprinkle with the reserved crumb mixture.

Makes 7 servings.

Toffee Pie Crust

1/2	cup sifted flour
1/4	teaspoon salt
1/2	teaspoon sugar
3	tablespoons shortening
1/3	cup finely chopped pecans
2	tablespoons brown sugar
1	ounce unsweetened chocolate, grated
1	tablespoon water
1/2	teaspoon vanilla extract

Sift the flour, salt and sugar into a bowl and mix well. Cut in the shortening until crumbly. Add the pecans, brown sugar and chocolate and mix well. Reserve 1 tablespoon of the crumb mixture. Add the water and vanilla to the remaining crumb mixture and mix well. Press into a greased 8-inch pie plate. Bake at 375 degrees for 15 minutes. Let stand until cool. Spread the reserved crumb mixture in a pan. Bake at 375 degrees for 5 minutes.

Gee Gee Steves
San Antonio, Texas

Apple Cheese

1 (16-ounce) can sliced apples, drained
1 cup sugar
3/4 cup self-rising flour
1/2 cup butter, softened
8 ounces Velveeta cheese, shredded

Spread the apples in a buttered 9x9-inch baking dish. Beat the sugar, flour, butter and cheese in a mixer bowl until blended, scraping the bowl occasionally. Spread over the apples. Bake at 350 degrees for 30 minutes or until light brown.
Makes 6 to 8 servings.

Marguerite Wilson
Brownwood, Texas

Apples Simply Prepared

3 organic apples, sliced
Juice of 1/2 large lemon
Freshly grated nutmeg to taste

Combine the apples and lemon juice in a bowl, tossing to coat. Sprinkle with nutmeg. Marinate, covered, in the refrigerator for 1 hour. Arrange the apple slices in a circle on a serving platter. Sprinkle with nutmeg. May intersperse slices of other colorful fresh fruit on the serving platter.
Makes 4 to 5 servings.

Mollie Gates
San Antonio, Texas

The strength of the Warm Springs Foundation lies not in this physical plant, which you see in operation or under construction here today, but in its human resources—the men and women from all walks of life, and from all sections of Texas, who make up this organization.

Ross Boothe, founding charter board member, deceased

Apple Squares

1 1/2   cups sugar
1/2   cup melted butter, cooled
2   eggs
1/2   teaspoon vanilla extract
2   cups whole wheat flour
2   teaspoons baking powder
1   teaspoon cinnamon
2   small Granny Smith apples, chopped
1/2   cup chopped nuts

Combine the sugar, butter, eggs and vanilla in a bowl and mix well. Combine the whole wheat flour, baking powder and cinnamon in a bowl and mix well. Stir into the sugar mixture. Add the apples and nuts and mix well. Spoon into a greased and floured 11x13-inch baking pan. Bake at 350 degrees for 30 minutes. Cut into squares while warm.

Makes 12 squares.

Michelle Flores
San Antonio, Texas

Brennan's Bananas Foster

2   tablespoons butter
4   small bananas, cut lengthwise into halves
2   tablespoons brown sugar
1/8   teaspoon cinnamon
1/2   cup rum
1   tablespoon banana liqueur
        Vanilla ice cream

Heat the butter in a skillet until melted. Add the bananas. Cook until brown. Sprinkle with the brown sugar and cinnamon. Stir in the rum and banana liqueur and mix well; ignite. Serve blazing with ice cream.

Makes 4 servings.

Bonnie Street
San Antonio, Texas

Caribbean Baked Bananas

Great for summer entertaining. Serve warm with a dollop of vanilla ice milk or frozen nonfat yogurt or serve chilled. It is also delicious spread on toast or served with pancakes or waffles for a brunch.

1/4	cup confectioners' sugar
1/4	cup flour
1	teaspoon cinnamon
3	large bananas, cut diagonally into 1-inch slices
1/4	cup dark rum
1/4	cup water
2	tablespoons dark brown sugar

Combine the confectioners' sugar, flour and cinnamon in a sealable plastic bag, shaking to mix. Add the banana slices, shaking to coat. Arrange the bananas in an 8x8-inch baking pan or a 5x9-inch loaf pan sprayed with nonstick cooking spray. Combine the rum, water and brown sugar in a bowl and mix well. Pour over the bananas. Bake at 350 degrees for 25 minutes or until golden brown. May prepare the bananas without rum by substituting 1/2 cup apple juice for the rum and water, reducing the brown sugar to 1 tablespoon and adding 1 teaspoon vanilla and 1/2 teaspoon rum extract.
    Makes 6 servings.

A Friend of Warm Springs

Banana Pudding

1	(12-ounce) package (about) vanilla wafers
4	or 5 bananas, sliced
2	(4-ounce) packages vanilla instant pudding mix
3	cups milk
1	(14-ounce) can sweetened condensed milk
8	ounces cream cheese, softened
8	ounces whipped topping

Line the bottom and sides of a 9x13-inch dish with vanilla wafers. Arrange the banana slices over the wafers, overlapping as needed. Prepare the pudding mix in a mixer bowl using 3 cups milk. Beat in the condensed milk and cream cheese until blended. Fold in the whipped topping. Pour over the bananas. Chill until serving time.
    Makes 12 to 15 servings.

Lillian Gohlke
Sheridan, Texas

Caramel Custard

1 cup sugar
1 tablespoon water
4 cups milk, boiling
1 cup sugar
1 vanilla bean
8 eggs, beaten

Combine 1 cup sugar and water in a saucepan. Bring to a boil. Boil for a few minutes or until the sugar dissolves and the mixture is caramel in color. Combine the milk and 1 cup sugar in a bowl, stirring until the sugar dissolves. Stir in the vanilla bean. Stir a small amount of the hot mixture into the eggs; stir the eggs into the hot mixture. Pour the caramel mixture into a mold. Spoon the custard into the mold. Place the mold in a larger pan; add hot water to reach halfway up the side of the mold. Bake at 350 degrees for 20 minutes. Remove the mold from the water bath. Let stand until cool. Invert onto a serving platter.

Makes 6 to 8 servings.

Catherine Spruce
Abilene, Texas

Bread Pudding

1	cup sugar
4	eggs
2½	cups milk
2	slices bread, cubed
¼	teaspoon cinnamon
1½	cups chopped apples
¼	cup chopped pecans

Beat the sugar and eggs in a bowl until blended. Stir in the milk, bread and cinnamon. Add the apples and pecans and mix well. Spoon into an 8x8-inch baking pan. Bake at 325 degrees until a knife inserted in the center comes out clean.

Makes 4 to 6 servings.

Verna Cunningham
Victoria, Texas

Cream Cheesecake

24	ounces cream cheese, softened
1	cup sugar
3	tablespoons flour
4	eggs, at room temperature
1	teaspoon vanilla extract
⅛	teaspoon salt
2	cups sour cream
6	tablespoons sugar
1	teaspoon almond extract

Beat the cream cheese, 1 cup sugar, flour, eggs, vanilla and salt in a mixer bowl until creamy, scraping the bowl occasionally. Spoon into a greased and floured springform pan. Bake at 350 degrees for 30 to 35 minutes. Let stand for 15 minutes or until cool. Spread with a mixture of the sour cream, 6 tablespoons sugar and almond extract. Bake for 10 minutes longer. Let stand until cool. Chill until serving time. Garnish with fruit or spread with pie filling of your choice.

Makes 12 to 14 servings.

Dean Coldeway
Yoakum, Texas

German Cheesecake

Great to serve either as a dessert or for breakfast.

1	(8-count) can crescent rolls
16	ounces cream cheese, softened
1	cup sugar
1	egg yolk
1	(8-count) can crescent rolls
1	egg white, lightly beaten
1/4	teaspoon sugar
1/4	teaspoon cinnamon
1/2	cup confectioners' sugar
1	tablespoon (about) milk
	Vanilla extract to taste
	Chopped nuts (optional)

Separate 1 can crescent roll dough into triangles. Pat over the bottom of a 9x9-inch baking dish, pressing edges to seal. Beat the cream cheese, 1 cup sugar and egg yolk in a mixer bowl until creamy. Spread over the prepared layer. Separate the remaining can crescent roll dough into triangles. Arrange the triangles over the top, pressing edges to seal. Brush with the egg white. Sprinkle with a mixture of 1/4 teaspoon sugar and cinnamon. Bake at 350 degrees for 45 minutes. Blend the confectioners' sugar with just enough milk in a bowl to make of drizzling consistency. Stir in the vanilla and nuts. Drizzle over the hot cheesecake.

Makes 6 to 8 servings.

Mary Tupacz
San Antonio, Texas

I can't look at her without thinking about it. She was just so lucky. So many people helped her out and supported us. We've told so many people about Warm Springs that even our friends and neighbors have gone there for treatment.

Lillian Simmons, parent of former brain-injury patient Kim Simmons, McCoy, Texas

No-Bake Pineapple Cheesecake

1	(3-ounce) package lemon gelatin
1 1/4	cups graham cracker crumbs
1/3	cup melted margarine
1/4	cup sugar
8	ounces cream cheese, softened
8	ounces whipped topping
1	cup sugar
1	(8-ounce) can crushed pineapple, drained
	Graham cracker crumbs

Prepare the gelatin using package directions for the speed set method. Let stand until partially set. Combine 1 1/4 cups graham cracker crumbs, margarine and 1/4 cup sugar in a bowl and mix well. Press the mixture using the back of a spoon over the bottom and sides of a 9x13-inch dish. Chill in the refrigerator. Beat the cream cheese, whipped topping, 1 cup sugar and gelatin in a mixer bowl until blended. Stir in the pineapple gradually. Spoon into the prepared dish. Sprinkle with graham cracker crumbs. Chill for 2 hours.

Makes 12 servings.

Donna R. Flores
Yorktown, Texas

Cream Dessert

1	(7-inch) angel food cake, cut into 1/4-inch slices
1	(14-ounce) can sweetened condensed milk
1	cup cold water
1	teaspoon almond extract
1	(4-ounce) package vanilla instant pudding mix
2	cups whipping cream, whipped
4	cups chopped fresh fruit

Arrange 1/2 of the cake slices in the bottom of a 9x13-inch dish. Combine the condensed milk, water and almond extract in a bowl and mix well. Add the pudding mix, beating until blended. Chill for 5 minutes. Fold in the whipped cream. Spoon 1/2 of the pudding mixture over the cake slices. Layer with the remaining cake slices and remaining pudding mixture. Top with the fruit. Chill for 4 hours or until set. Cut into squares to serve. May substitute cherry pie filling for the fresh fruit; do not use canned fruit.

Makes 12 servings.

Kermit and Corinne Rudloff
Brenham, Texas

Frozen Peppermint Cheesecake

- 1 (14-ounce) can sweetened condensed milk
- 8 ounces cream cheese, softened
- 1 cup crushed peppermint candy
- 2 cups whipping cream, whipped
- Red food coloring
- 1 (9-inch) chocolate graham cracker pie shell

Beat the condensed milk and cream cheese in a bowl until blended. Stir in the peppermint candy. Fold in the whipped cream and red food coloring. Spoon into the pie shell. Freeze until set.

Makes 6 to 8 servings.

Susan Zakrzewski
San Antonio, Texas

Dump Cake

- 1 (21-ounce) can cherry pie filling
- 1 (16-ounce) can crushed pineapple, drained
- 1 (2-layer) package yellow cake mix
- 1 cup melted butter
- Shredded coconut
- Chopped pecans

Layer the pie filling, pineapple and cake mix in a 9x13-inch baking pan. Drizzle with the butter. Sprinkle with coconut and pecans. Bake at 325 degrees for 40 minutes.

Makes 8 to 10 servings.

Skipper Truitt
Aransas Pass, Texas

My most favorite therapist (Connie Pesek) helped me make "Dump Cake" while I was at Gonzales Warm Springs Rehabilitation Hospital about fourteen years ago. Actually, the most important ingredient was love. Thanks!

Skipper Truitt, former patient,
Aransas Pass, Texas

Triple Orange Delight

1 package angel food cake mix, prepared
2 (11-ounce) cans mandarin oranges
2 (3-ounce) packages orange gelatin
1 quart orange sherbet
12 ounces whipped topping
  Whipped topping to taste
  Fresh mint leaves

Brush the loose crumbs from the cake. Cut or tear the cake into bite-size pieces. Drain the mandarin oranges, reserving 1 cup of the juice. Reserve 12 to 16 sections. Cut the remaining orange sections into bite-size pieces. Bring the reserved juice to a boil in a saucepan. Add the gelatin, stirring until dissolved. Combine the juice mixture and sherbet in a bowl, stirring until the sherbet melts. Fold in 12 ounces whipped topping. Layer the cake, orange pieces and sherbet mixture 1/2 at a time in a 9x13-inch dish. Chill, covered, for 8 to 10 hours. Cut into squares. Top each serving with additional whipped topping, 1 reserved mandarin orange section and a mint leaf.

Makes 12 to 16 servings.

Betty J. Rogers
San Antonio, Texas

Andrew is an avid sports fan. Wheelchair Sports gives him the opportunity to be a true competitor instead of an observer.

David McAllister Family, 1997 Wheelchair Sports Family of the Year, San Antonio, Texas

Punch Bowl Trifle

1	(2-layer) package yellow cake mix
3	(4-ounce) packages vanilla instant pudding mix
6	cups milk
4	bananas, sliced
2	tablespoons (about) lemon juice
1	(21-ounce) can cherry pie filling
1	(16-ounce) can pineapple chunks, drained
16	ounces whipped topping
	Chopped pecans
	Shredded coconut

Prepare and bake the cake mix according to the package directions in any size pan. Cool the cake in the pan for 10 minutes. Invert onto a wire rack to cool completely. Cut the cake into cubes. Prepare the pudding mix with the milk according to the package directions. Brush the banana slices with lemon juice to prevent browning. Layer half the cake cubes in a punch bowl or other large clear glass bowl. Add layers of half the pie filling, half the pineapple chunks, half the bananas and half the whipped topping. Repeat the layers. Top with pecans and coconut. Chill until serving time.

Variation: Sprinkle the pecans and coconut between the layers as well as on the top.

Makes variable servings.

Vicki Fisher
New Braunfels, Texas

Oreo Cookie Torte

1	(15-ounce) package Oreo cookies
1/3	cup melted margarine
1/2	gallon vanilla ice cream, sliced
1	small can chocolate syrup
8	ounces whipped topping

Crush the Oreo cookies. Reserve 2 cups of the crumbs. Combine the margarine with the remaining cookie crumbs in a bowl and mix well. Press into a 9x13-inch dish. Layer the ice cream, chocolate syrup and whipped topping in the prepared dish. Sprinkle with the reserved cookie crumbs. Freeze, covered, until set. Let stand at room temperature for 10 minutes before slicing.

Makes 8 servings.

Deanne Kindred
San Antonio, Texas

Easy Fruit Cobbler

5	tablespoons plus 1 teaspoon margarine
1	cup sugar
1	cup flour
1	teaspoon baking powder
1/2	teaspoon salt (optional)
2/3	cup milk
1	teaspoon vanilla extract
2	cups canned or cooked fruit of choice

Heat the margarine in a 1 1/2-quart baking dish until melted. Combine the sugar, flour, baking powder and salt in a bowl and mix well. Stir in the milk and vanilla. Spoon into the prepared dish. Top with the fruit. Bake at 325 degrees for 1 hour. Serve hot or at room temperature.

Makes 8 servings.

Elvera Jaks
Shiner, Texas

Rehab is hard work. Try not to get frustrated. Never get to the point where you think you can't make any more progress. Just remember that every little goal reached is a step toward a bigger goal. There's always a little bit more that you can do, if you try.

Troy Johnston, former spinal-cord-injury patient, San Marcos, Texas

Easy Fruit Salad Dessert

3	bananas, sliced
1	cup sliced strawberries
1	green apple, cored, chopped
1	(11-ounce) can mandarin oranges, drained
2	kiwifruit, peeled, chopped
1	(16-ounce) can sliced peaches, drained
1	(8-ounce) carton raspberry yogurt

Combine the bananas, strawberries, apple, mandarin oranges, kiwifruit and peaches in a bowl. Add the yogurt and mix gently until the fruit is coated. Chill, covered, for 30 to 60 minutes. Garnish with additional strawberries and kiwifruit.

Variation: Substitute or add your favorite fruit as desired. Substitute other flavored yogurt to taste or select the colors of fruit and/or yogurt to enhance the appearance of the dessert or your table setting.

Makes 6 to 8 servings.

Pam Wimberley
Stillwater, Oklahoma

Nutty Peach Crisp

1	(29-ounce) can sliced peaches
1	(2-layer) package butter cake mix
½	cup melted butter
1	cup flaked coconut
1	cup chopped pecans

Layer the undrained peaches, cake mix, butter, coconut and pecans in the order listed in a greased 9x13-inch baking pan. Bake at 325 degrees for 55 to 60 minutes. Let stand for 15 minutes before serving. Serve warm or at room temperature with whipped cream or ice cream.

Makes 12 to 15 servings.

Linda E. Patteson
Nixon, Texas

So-Easy Peach Crisp

2	(28-ounce) cans sliced peaches
2	cups flour
2	cups sugar
½	cup margarine
	Cinnamon to taste

Drain the peaches, reserving the juice. Pour the peach slices into a 9x13-inch baking dish sprayed with nonstick cooking spray. Combine the flour and sugar in a bowl. Cut in the margarine until crumbly. Spread the flour mixture evenly over the peaches. Sprinkle with cinnamon. Bake at 350 degrees for 35 to 40 minutes or until brown. May spoon small amounts of the reserved juice over the topping during the baking process.

Makes 8 servings.

Dorothy Williamson
San Marcos, Texas

Sweet Potato Crisp

2	(29-ounce) cans sweet potatoes or yams
1	cup milk
1	cup sugar
4	eggs
2	tablespoons vanilla extract
1/4	cup melted butter or margarine
	Pecan Topping

Drain the sweet potatoes and mash in a large bowl. Add the milk, sugar, eggs, vanilla and butter and mix until smooth. Pour the mixture into a greased 9x13-inch baking dish. Spread the Pecan Topping over the sweet potato mixture. Bake at 325 degrees for 1 hour.

Makes 12 or more servings.

Pecan Topping

1	cup flour
2	cups packed brown sugar
1	cup butter or margarine, softened
2	cups chopped pecans

Combine the flour and brown sugar in a bowl and mix well. Cut in the butter until crumbly. Add the pecans and mix well.

Leslie Guess
San Antonio, Texas

Warm Springs has helped a lot. When I first came here, I could not bathe, shave, or dress myself. In only a few weeks, I've been able to strengthen my left side, and now I plan to go back to work some time after I return home. I'm very excited to have been able to do this. I definitely plan to tell others about my rehabilitation here in the United States at Warm Springs.

Douglas Reymi, former stroke patient, Venezuela (referred to Gonzales Warm Springs through Venezuelan friends with friends living in Victoria, Texas)

About the Artist – Beth Eidelberg

Beth Eidelberg was born in San Antonio where her devotion to art developed in early childhood. She remembers beginning her artistic pursuits at the age of five, studying as a young girl at the Little House School of Art and Witte Museum. Her further studies at Monticello College (Alton, Illinois), which she attended on a fine arts scholarship, San Antonio Art Institute, University of Texas at San Antonio, and Albert Glassell School of Fine Arts (Houston) have been a continuing educational experience. Eidelberg's oils and watercolors reflect not only her regional surroundings of Texas and the Southwest, but also her extensive travels abroad.

Eidelberg has exhibited extensively since her first one-person show at La Sirena in 1964. She has shown regularly in the annual juried competitions of the Texas Watercolor Society, San Antonio Art League, San Antonio Watercolor Group, Art League of Houston, Watercolor Art Society of Houston, and Western Federation of Watercolor Societies. Over her thirty-year career, she has received numerous recognitions and awards from the American Watercolor Society, National Academy of Design in New York, Southern Watercolor Society Annual, Texas Watercolor Society, San Antonio Watercolor Group, Western Federation of Watercolor Societies, Watercolor Art Society (Houston), and the San Antonio Art League. Her work has been published by the New York Graphic Society and was featured in *American Artist* magazine. Galleries throughout the Southwest have represented her work, which is also included in numerous private and corporate collections. In 1990, the artist was named Artist of the Year by the San Antonio Art League, truly a prestigious honor.

Community service has distinguished the artist throughout her career. She has completed a mural for the Ronald McDonald House and served by invitation as the poster artist for the San Antonio Museum Association, San Antonio Symphony Designers Showcase, San Antonio Performing Arts Association, Alamo Kiwanis and First Presbyterian Church. She was selected to depict the state capitol for the official state capitol *Centennial Celebration* booklet in 1988. She also has served on numerous arts-related boards and committees, demonstrating the strong commitment she feels to her city and profession.

One enters with pleasure the untroubled, unshadowed world of Beth Eidelberg, whose clear watercolors are exacting yet reassuring. To be named Artist of the Year by the San Antonio Art League signifies not only distinguished performance, but sustained quality. One good painting does not constitute an honored exhibition. Ms. Eidelberg's continued production, her endless list of exhibitions and honors testify to the presence of a serious, consistent, and skillful artist. San Antonio and Texas remain strongholds of the traditions of transparent watercolor painting, and Beth Eidelberg is in the first rank of its practitioners.

The late John Palmer Leeper
Director Emeritus
Marion Koogler McNay Art Museum

Index

APPETIZERS. *See also* Dips; Spreads
Armadillo Eggs, 20
Cheese Rings, 18
E-Z Party Pecans, 21
Hot Crab Meat Ramekins, 19
Pinwheels, 21

APPLE
Apple Cake, 106
Apple Cheese, 139
Apple Crunch Cake, 107
Applesauce Fruitcake, 108
Applesauce Spice Cake, 109
Apple Squares, 140
Apples Simply Prepared, 139
Caramel Crunch Apple Pie, 134
Curried Spinach and Apple Spread, 18
Easy Fruit Salad Dessert, 151
Floating Chops with Fruit-Filled Squash, 54
Waldorf Salad, 33

APRICOT
Apricot Nectar Cake, 110
Apricot Pineapple Salad, 31

ARTICHOKES
Artichoke Dip, 14
Hot and Spicy Shrimp Dip, 15
Libby's Dip, 15
Tuscan Fettuccini with Artichokes Stefano, 94
Zesty Oregano Chicken, 70

BANANA
Banana Cake, 111
Banana Pudding, 141
Blueberry Banana Snack Cake, 112
Brennan's Bananas Foster, 140
Caribbean Baked Bananas, 141
Easy Fruit Salad Dessert, 151
Frosted Salad, 31
Old-Fashioned Banana Cake, 113

BEANS
Black Bean Salad, 38
Black-Eyed Peas and Corn Bread Casserole, 47
Green Bean Casserole, 85
Mexican Layered Dip, 16
Pancho Villa's Dip, 14
Pinto Bean Fiesta Fudge, 123
Pinto Bean Pie, 136
Roasted Green Beans, 86

BEEF. *See also* Ground Beef
Beef Paprika, 45
Borsch, 24
Chili Verde, 51
Dynamite Marinade, 45
Five-Hour Stew, 46
Lemon Herb Pot Roast, 44

BREADS. *See also* Coffee Cakes; Muffins
Gingerbread, 113
Greek Bread, 100
Lakota Indian Fry Bread, 100
Old-Fashioned Walnut Bread, 101
Pumpkin Bread, 101

CAKES. *See also* Coffee Cakes
Apple Cake, 106
Apple Crunch Cake, 107
Applesauce Fruitcake, 108
Applesauce Spice Cake, 109
Apricot Nectar Cake, 110
Banana Cake, 111
Best-Ever Chocolate Cake, 114
Blueberry Banana Snack Cake, 112
Gingerbread, 113
Lemon Cake, 115
Old-Fashioned Banana Cake, 113
Orange Cake, 116
Orange Christmas Cake, 117
Pineapple Cake, 119
Pineapple Upside-Down Cake, 118
Rum Cake, 120
Strawberry Cake, 121
Texas Vanilla Sheet Cake, 122

CANDY
Divinity, 123
Microwave Peanut Brittle, 123
Pinto Bean Fiesta Fudge, 123

CARROT
Carrots Amandine, 82
Chicken and Carrot Salad, 33
Copper Coins, 82

CAULIFLOWER
Broccoli and Cauliflower Salad, 37
Cheesy Cauliflower, 83

CHEESECAKES
Cream Cheesecake, 143
Frozen Peppermint Cheesecake, 147
German Cheesecake, 144
No-Bake Pineapple Cheesecake, 145

CHICKEN
All-In-One, 57
Aunt Patty's Sopa, 62
Cheese and Tomato Toss, 95
Chicken à la Français, 60
Chicken and Carrot Salad, 33
Chicken and Dumplings, 58
Chicken and Spaghetti, 67
Chicken and Spaghetti in Wine Sauce, 68
Chicken Creole, 59
Chicken Potpie, 63
Chicken with Rice, 64
Dynamite Marinade, 45
Easy Hot Chicken Salad, 65
Green Enchiladas, 67
Honey Mustard Chicken, 61
Hot Chicken Salad, 66
Little Red Hen, 61
Wild Rice Chicken Salad, 35
Yorkshire Chicken, 69
Zesty Oregano Chicken, 70

CHOCOLATE
Best-Ever Chocolate Cake, 114
Blarney Kisses, 126
Chocolate Frosting, 114
English Toffee Pie, 138

Index

Favorite Oatmeal
  Cookies, 131
Macadamia Nut and
  White Chocolate
  Cookies, 128
Oreo Cookie Torte, 150
Toffee Pie Crust, 138

COFFEE CAKES
Cherry Cheese Coffee
  Cake, 99
Favorite Coffee Cake, 99

COOKIES
Belgian Almond
  Cookies, 124
Black-Skillet
  Brownies, 125
Blarney Kisses, 126
Cheater Cookies, 129
Crunchy Nut
  Cookies, 127
Favorite Oatmeal
  Cookies, 131
Forgotten Cookies, 129
Macadamia Nut and
  White Chocolate
  Cookies, 128
Millionaire Squares, 130
Orange Slice Bars, 133
Teacakes, 132
World's Best Cookies, 133

CORN
Corn and Noodle
  Casserole, 84
Corn Casserole, 85
Hudson's on the Bend
  Corn Pudding, 83
White Corn Chowder, 26

DESSERTS. *See also* Cakes;
  Candy; Cookies; Pies
Apple Cheese, 139

Apple Squares, 140
Apples Simply
  Prepared, 139
Black-Skillet
  Brownies, 125
Brennan's Bananas
  Foster, 140
Caribbean Baked
  Bananas, 141
Cream Dessert, 146
Dump Cake, 147
Easy Fruit Cobbler, 150
Easy Fruit Salad
  Dessert, 151
Nutty Peach Crisp, 152
Oreo Cookie Torte, 150
Punch Bowl Trifle, 149
So-Easy Peach
  Crisp, 152
Sweet Potato Crisp, 153
Triple Orange
  Delight, 148

DIPS
Artichoke Dip, 14
Hot and Spicy Shrimp
  Dip, 15
Libby's Dip, 15
Mexican Layered Dip, 16
Pancho Villa's Dip, 14

EGG DISHES
Chili Cheese Casserole, 93
Sour Cream Onion Pie, 91

FISH
Dynamite Marinade, 45
Grilled Swordfish, 79
Pescado Picante, 73
Tuna Noodle Crisp, 74

FROSTINGS/GLAZES
Butter Frosting, 116
Chocolate Frosting, 114

Cream Cheese
  Frosting, 122
Lemon Glaze, 115
Mint Frosting, 126
Rum Glaze, 120
Strawberry Frosting, 121

GROUND BEEF
Black-Eyed Peas and Corn
  Bread Casserole, 47
Green Enchiladas, 67
Mexican Chef Salad, 36
Mother's Tamale Pie, 49
Slow-Cooker Soup, 28
Stroganoff Burgers, 48
Taco Soup, 29
Texas Tech Chili, 50

LAMB
Grilled Leg of Lamb, 56

MUFFINS
Morning Glory
  Muffins, 102
Six-Week Muffins, 103

ORANGE
Orange Cake, 116
Orange Christmas
  Cake, 117
Triple Orange
  Delight, 148

PASTA
Cheese and Tomato
  Toss, 95
Chicken and Spaghetti, 67
Chicken and Spaghetti in
  Wine Sauce, 68
Primavera Salad, 34
Sun-Dried Tomato
  Pesto, 95
Tuscan Fettuccini with
  Artichokes Stefano, 94

PEACH
Nutty Peach Crisp, 152
So-Easy Peach
  Crisp, 152

PIES
Caramel Crunch Apple
  Pie, 134
English Toffee Pie, 138
Lemon Pie, 136
Pinto Bean Pie, 136
Pumpkin Pie, 137
Strawberry Pie, 137
Toffee Pie Crust, 138

PIES, COCONUT
Coconut Cream
  Pie, 135
Crustless Coconut
  Pie, 135
Impossible Pie, 135

PINEAPPLE
Apricot Pineapple
  Salad, 31
No-Bake Pineapple
  Cheesecake, 145
Pineapple Cake, 119
Pineapple Upside-Down
  Cake, 118

PORK. *See also* Sausage
Chili Verde, 51
Dynamite Marinade, 45
Floating Chops with Fruit-
  Filled Squash, 54
Jamaican Spiced Pork
  Tenderloin with Sweet
  Potato Purée, 53
Orange-Glazed Pork
  Roast, 52
Rosemary-and-Serrano-
  Roasted Pork
  Tenderloin, 55

POTATO
  Barbecue Potatoes, 86
  Delicious Potatoes, 87
  Easy New Potatoes, 87
  Hearty Potato
    Soup, 27
  Olive Oil Mashed
    Potatoes, 87

PUDDINGS
  Banana Pudding, 141
  Bread Pudding, 143
  Caramel Custard, 142

RICE. *See also* Salads, Rice
  Jalapeño Rice, 98
  Spanish Rice, 96

SALAD DRESSINGS
  Versatile Vinaigrette, 34
  Western Salad
    Dressing, 41

SALADS, FRUIT
  Apricot Pineapple
    Salad, 31
  Frosted Salad, 31
  Mango Salad, 32
  Royal Pear Salad, 32
  Waldorf Salad, 33

SALADS, MAIN DISH
  Chicken and Carrot
    Salad, 33
  Mexican Chef Salad, 36
  Primavera Salad, 34
  Wild Rice Chicken
    Salad, 35

SALADS, RICE
  E-Z Rice Salad, 37
  Wild Rice Chicken
    Salad, 35

SALADS, VEGETABLE
  Black Bean Salad, 38
  Broccoli and Cauliflower
    Salad, 37
  German Slaw, 39
  Overnight Vegetable
    Salad, 39
  Seven-Layer Salad, 40
  Tomato Vegetable Aspic
    Salad, 41

SAUCES
  Wine Sauce, 56

SAUSAGE
  Armadillo Eggs, 20
  Sausage Dressing, 97
  Texas Tech Chili, 50

SEAFOOD. *See also* Fish;
    Shrimp
  Chilled Clam Soup, 27
  Crawfish Etouffée, 72
  Hot Crab Meat
    Ramekins, 19

SHRIMP
  Dynamite Marinade, 45
  Grilled Shrimp and
    Vegetables, 78
  Hot and Spicy Shrimp
    Dip, 15
  Rio Grande Shrimp, 77

  Shrimp and Lobster with
    Wild Rice, 76
  Shrimp Conchiglia, 75
  Shrimp in Sour Cream, 77
  Shrimp Mold, 18
  Spicy Camp Shrimp, 75
  Tuscan Fettuccini with
    Artichokes Stefano, 94

SIDE DISHES
  Baked Grits, 98
  Jalapeño Rice, 98
  Sausage Dressing, 97
  Spanish Rice, 96

SIDE DISHES, FRUIT
  Baked Fruit, 93
  Hot Fruit Compote, 92

SNACKS. *See* Appetizers

SOUPS
  Borsch, 24
  Canadian Cheese
    Soup, 25
  Chilled Clam Soup, 27
  Hearty Potato Soup, 27
  Mexican Cream Soup, 28
  Slow-Cooker Soup, 28
  Sopa de Chayote, 30
  Taco Soup, 29
  White Corn Chowder, 26

SPINACH
  Curried Spinach and
    Apple Spread, 18
  Primavera Salad, 34
  Spinach Casserole, 88

SPREADS
  Cheese Balls, 17
  Curried Spinach and
    Apple Spread, 18
  Shrimp Mold, 18

SQUASH
  Baked Squash Daniel, 89
  Floating Chops with Fruit-
    Filled Squash, 54

STRAWBERRY
  Easy Fruit Salad
    Dessert, 151
  Strawberry Cake, 121
  Strawberry Frosting, 121
  Strawberry Pie, 137

SWEET POTATO
  Sweet Potato Crisp, 153
  Sweet Potato Purée, 53

TURKEY
  Aunt Patty's Sopa, 62
  Marinated Turkey, 71
  Primavera Salad, 34

VEGETABLES. *See also*
    Artichokes; Beans;
    Carrot; Cauliflower;
    Corn; Potato; Salads,
    Vegetable; Spinach
  Sour Cream Onion Pie, 91
  Vegetable Pie, 90

Order Forms

Recipes for Success

Warm Springs Rehabilitation Foundation, Inc.
909 NE Loop 410, Suite 500, San Antonio, Texas 78209
1-800-457-0777 / www.warmsprings.org

Please send me _____ copies of *Recipes for Success* @ $17.95 each $ _____
add postage and handling @ $ 3.00 each $ _____
Texas residents add sales tax @ $ 1.39 each $ _____
Total $ _____

❑ Check   ❑ AMEX   ❑ MasterCard   ❑ VISA   Card Number _____

Expiration Date _____   Signature _____

Name _____   Phone (____) _____

Address _____

City _____ State _____ Zip _____

Please make checks payable to Warm Springs Rehabilitation Foundation, Inc.

Recipes for Success

Warm Springs Rehabilitation Foundation, Inc.
909 NE Loop 410, Suite 500, San Antonio, Texas 78209
1-800-457-0777 / www.warmsprings.org

Please send me _____ copies of *Recipes for Success* @ $17.95 each $ _____
add postage and handling @ $ 3.00 each $ _____
Texas residents add sales tax @ $ 1.39 each $ _____
Total $ _____

❑ Check   ❑ AMEX   ❑ MasterCard   ❑ VISA   Card Number _____

Expiration Date _____   Signature _____

Name _____   Phone (____) _____

Address _____

City _____ State _____ Zip _____

Please make checks payable to Warm Springs Rehabilitation Foundation, Inc.

Photocopies will be accepted.